THE GOSPEL PROJECT

SAVED

Life in the Face of Death

Ed Stetzer
Trevin Wax

LifeWay Press®
Nashville, Tennessee

Item: 005695954
ISBN: 978-1-4300-3676-0
Dewey decimal classification number: 234
Subject heading: SALVATION \ FAITH \ GRACE (THEOLOGY)

We believe that the Bible has God for its author; salvation for its end; and truth, without any mixture of error, for its matter and that all Scripture is totally true and trustworthy. To review LifeWay's doctrinal guideline, please visit *www.lifeway.com/doctrinalguideline.*

For ordering or inquiries, visit *www.lifeway.com;* write LifeWay Small Groups; One LifeWay Plaza; Nashville, TN 37234-0152; or call toll free (800) 458-2772.

Printed in the United States of America.

Adult Ministry Publishing
LifeWay Church Resources
One LifeWay Plaza
Nashville, Tennessee 37234-0152

TABLE OF CONTENTS

ABOUT THE GOSPEL PROJECT

Some people see the Bible as a collection of stories with morals for life application. But it's so much more. Sure, the Bible has some stories in it, but it's also full of poetry, history, codes of law and civilization, songs, prophecy, letters—even a love letter. When you tie it all together, something remarkable happens. A story is revealed. One story. The story of redemption through Jesus. This is *The Gospel Project.*

When we begin to see the Bible as the story of redemption through Jesus Christ, God's plan to rescue the world from sin and death, our perspective changes. We no longer look primarily for what the Bible says about us but instead see what it tells us about God and what He has done. After all, it's the gospel that saves us, and when we encounter Jesus in the pages of Scripture, the gospel works on us, transforming us into His image. *We become God's gospel project.*

ABOUT THE WRITERS

Trevin Wax is managing editor for *The Gospel Project* and the author of *Clear Winter Nights*, *Gospel-Centered Teaching*, and *Counterfeit Gospels*. He has served in pastoral roles in the United States and Romania. He and his wife, Corina, reside in Middle Tennessee with their three children.

Ed Stetzer is the president of LifeWay Research Division, a prolific author, and well-known conference and seminar leader. He is the author of "The Exchange," a blog with *Christianity Today*. In addition to being the executive editor of *The Gospel Project*, he is the lead pastor of Grace Church in Hendersonville, TN, a congregation he planted in 2011.

Barry Cram adapted this material for use with small groups.

HOW TO USE THIS STUDY

Welcome to *The Gospel Project*, a gospel-centered small-group study that dives deep into the things of God, lifts up Jesus, focuses on the grand story of Scripture, and drives participants to be on mission. This small-group Bible study provides opportunities to study the Bible and to encounter the living Christ. *The Gospel Project* provides you with tools and resources to purposefully study God's Word and to grow in the faith and knowledge of God's Son. And what's more, you can do so in the company of others, encouraging and building up one another. Here are some things to remember that will help you maximize the usefulness of this resource:

GATHER A GROUP. We grow in the faith best in community with other believers, as we love, encourage, correct, and challenge one another. The life of a disciple of Christ was never meant to be lived alone, in isolation.

PRAY. Pray regularly for your group members.

PREPARE. This resource includes the Bible study content, three devotionals, and discussion questions for each session. Work through the session and devotionals in preparation for each group session. Take notes and record your own questions. Also consider the follow-up questions so you are ready to participate in and add to the discussion, bringing up your own notes and questions where appropriate.

RESOURCE YOURSELF. Make good use of the additional resources available on the Web at *www.gospelproject.com/additionalresources* and search for this specific title. Download a podcast. Read a blog post. Be intentional about learning from others in the faith. For tips on how to better lead groups or additional ideas for leading this Bible study, visit: *www.ministrygrid.com/web/thegospelproject.*

GROUP TIME. Gather together with your group to discuss the session and devotional content. Work through the follow-up questions and your own questions. Discuss the material and the implications for the lives of believers and the mission to which we have been called.

OVERFLOW. Remember … *The Gospel Project* is not just a Bible study. *We* are the project. The gospel is working on us. Don't let your preparation time be simply about the content. Let the truths of God's Word soak in as you study. Let God work on your heart first, and then pray that He will change the hearts of the other people in your group.

Session 1

Because We Are Chosen

The ultimate final cause of our election is that the immense goodness of God and the righteousness of Christ offered to everyone should be everywhere magnified and exalted, not because God has any need of our praise but because by our praise many come to the salvation and blessedness that he offers to all.[1]

MARTIN BUCER

INDIVIDUAL STUDY

Even if you know absolutely nothing about football, you could watch a little league game and pick up on the fundamentals. You'd get the gist, right? There are two teams and one ball. Each team gets a few chances to advance the football and score a touchdown. And then they take turns. Oh, and they tackle each other, too. Simple, sweet, and very enjoyable—especially if your son or grandson is playing on the team!

But if you were to be invited to a college football game, you would get more than just the fundamentals. You would gain an entire experience! The massive stadium, the thousands of fans, the history behind the rivalry—this is where your perspective would change a great deal. You would be forced to see the bigger picture.

Describe a time in your life when you gained a bigger vision of something important. In what ways did that change your attitude, emotions, and behavior?

Sometimes we cling to a very small and simple version of Christianity: "If I just ask for forgiveness and I'm a good person, I go to heaven when I die." For some, that is the entire story. It's short and sweet. But we need to gain a bigger picture—a bigger vision—of how God is working His plan in Christ for our good and for His glory. When we understand this truth, our experience with God expands. It changes everything.

Those who are in Christ have been chosen by God. Far from leading to pride or never-ending debates, the doctrine of election is a spiritual blessing in Christ. It humbles us, assures us, and leads us to give all glory and praise to our missional God. When we understand the Bible's teaching on election, we're able to see the big picture of salvation from God's perspective. God is at work in Christ, working out our salvation for His glory and the furthering of His mission.

Throughout the week engage these daily study sections on your own. Each of these examines what it means to be chosen by God. There are three daily readings to prepare you before your group meets for this session. Interact with the Scriptures, and be ready to interact with your small group.

1 Election Means God Chose Us

[3] Praise the God and Father of our Lord Jesus Christ, who has blessed
us in Christ with every spiritual blessing in the heavens. [4] For He chose
us in Him, before the foundation of the world, to be holy and blameless
in His sight. In love [5] He predestined us to be adopted through Jesus
Christ for Himself, according to His favor and will, [6] to the praise of
His glorious grace that He favored us with in the Beloved.

EPHESIANS 1:3-6

In verse 4 we find what's called the *doctrine of election*—God elects (or chooses) us in Christ. This doctrine can easily make people nervous for many reasons. But it doesn't have to. Think of it this way. Remember when we were kids, and there was a going to be a game played with two teams? The two best players were captains, and they would pick their teammates—one by one. At some point, everyone was picked—even the worst players.

Well, that's what this passage teaches us—except there are no "worst" players. We're all sinners, but God chose us in Christ before the foundation of the world "to be holy and blameless in His sight" (v.4). God picked us, and Scripture is clear that God did so not because of us but in spite of us (see 1 Cor. 1:26-31).

How does it feel to be picked for something? How do you respond to this biblical truth that God picked you in Christ to be holy and blameless?

We can try to figure out why God would choose us, but to a certain degree, this will always seem mysterious. So mysterious, in fact, that good biblical Christians offer different explanations.

Review these views of election:

Conditional Election. Some people say election is based on God's foreknowledge of one's faith; in other words, election is conditional depending on a person's choice. Since God is omniscient (all-knowing), He knows all things before they happen, even from eternity past. Therefore, His choice to number someone among the elect is because He knew that person would respond to the gospel in faith and persevere in holy living.

Unconditional Election. Others say God chooses the elect unconditionally, or apart from any consideration of a person's actions, whether good or bad. God, being omniscient, simply chooses some to come to faith in Christ and be saved, without regard to merit or works. This displays His sovereignty, but we can't know why He might choose one person over another.

Corporate Election. Still others understand God's election to mean He chose a class of people—all those who would trust in Christ for salvation, or all those who are "in Christ" (v.3). In this perspective, individuals themselves are not the elect but a group is chosen by God. This believing community has been chosen to receive the promises and spiritual blessings that come through Jesus. It's argued that corporate election in the New Testament corresponds to the corporate election of the nation of Israel in the Old Testament.

If we're honest, we'll recognize how undeserving we are no matter which one of these views we lean toward. There is no cause for boasting. For His electing purpose, we should thank God: "But we must always thank God for you, brothers loved by the Lord, because from the beginning God has chosen you for salvation through sanctification by the Spirit and through belief in the truth" (2 Thess. 2:13).

How does God's choosing you in Christ before the foundation of the world encourage you to live a holy and blameless life in God's sight?

2 Election Means God Has a Plan

[5] He predestined us to be adopted through Jesus Christ
for Himself, according to His favor and will.
EPHESIANS 1:5

Predestination is a biblical word, but what does it mean? Is it scary? Is it controversial? It shouldn't be because it's a function of God's love. Nothing should be scary or controversial about that.

If you want to make predestination simple, here it is. Theologian J. I. Packer offers three words. "God saves sinners."[2] That includes all of us. That's it. By God's initiative, God does the saving. That doesn't mean we're not responsible to respond to Him. But God saves sinners for His glory so we can say, "God, thank You for saving me. May You receive the glory, the honor, and the praise."

God has a plan for you: you're going to be like Jesus. God looked before you were ever born. He saw you receiving Christ as your personal Savior and Lord. He said, "That one's going to be like Jesus." ... If you're predestined to be like Jesus, *of course* you will be like Jesus. What is foreknown in heaven cannot be annulled by hell. It's predestined; *it is settled!*[3]

ADRIAN ROGERS

What we must point out, however, is that in order to fully communicate God's Word, we must respond to God's electing, predestining work. In the original Greek translation, Ephesians 1:3-14 is one long sentence. It says we're elected and predestined, and when we believe, we're sealed with the Holy Spirit. Ephesians 1:13 says, "When you heard the message of truth, the gospel of your salvation, and when you believed in Him, you were also sealed with the promised Holy Spirit."

Let's look at some other passages that speak of God's plans. In Jeremiah 1:5, God told Jeremiah, "I chose you before I formed you in the womb; I set you apart before you were born. I appointed you a prophet to the nations." In Romans 8:29, Paul wrote, "For those He foreknew He also predestined to be conformed to the image of His Son, so that He would be the firstborn among many brothers." In Ephesians 1:11, Paul also said, "We have also received an inheritance in Him, predestined according to the purpose of the One who works out everything in agreement with the decision of His will."

How are you affected by the truth that your salvation isn't an accident but the result of God's plan?

Did you know that, according to the New Testament, all Christians are adopted? Nobody has ever been born into God's family; we've all been adopted. When God chose us, He made a decision about us ahead of time—to bring us into His family because having us in His family brings Him pleasure. He has redeemed us from slavery and adopted us as His children because He loves us and He delights in us.

Galatians 4:4-7 makes this clear:

> 4 When the time came to completion, God sent His Son, born of a woman,
> born under the law, 5 to redeem those under the law, so that we might
> receive adoption as sons. 6 And because you are sons, God has sent the
> Spirit of His Son into our hearts, crying, "*Abba*, Father!" So you are no
> longer a slave but a son, and if a son, then an heir through God.

The inheritance of God is ours through our adoption as His children. Jesus told His disciples, "You did not choose Me, but I chose you. I appointed you that you should go out and produce fruit and that your fruit should remain, so that whatever you ask the Father in My name, He will give you" (John 15:16). The plan of God, the mission of God, to send His Son to save sinners translates into a plan of action for His adopted children. We've been appointed to go out and produce fruit that will last—to proclaim the good news that Jesus came to seek and save the lost in order that the lost may be found.

What are some specific actions that would reflect the blessing of your adoption through Christ into God's family?

3 Election is About God's Glory

[3] Praise the God and Father of our Lord Jesus Christ, who has blessed us in Christ with every spiritual blessing in the heavens. … [6] to the praise of His glorious grace that He favored us with in the Beloved.
EPHESIANS 1:3,6

The first and last thing we see in this passage is a focus on God. When we consider how God has blessed us, it's not hard to see why we should want to bless Him. The Scripture says He's blessed us "with every spiritual blessing." Every good gift "in the heavens" has been granted to us through the greatest gift of all—Jesus Christ. When we're "in Christ," it's as if we're already raised from the dead and seated on a heavenly throne along with our Savior (see Eph. 2:6). We're blessed beyond measure because we're in Christ. How can we not be grateful, thankful, and overflowing with blessing toward the One who blesses us in Christ?

What are some examples of spiritual blessings we receive from Christ? How do these spiritual blessings encourage you to praise God?

Finally, we arrive at the purpose for God's electing work. It doesn't revolve around us, but it does include us. We've hinted at this before, but now Scripture lays it out. The focus here is God's glory.

Election helps us see how big God really is. Sometimes we can become satisfied with a small faith—like it's just about us. But with this doctrine in view, we can't say, "Look at me." We must say, "Look at God!" The God of all the universe is our Father—He adopted us! In love He predestined us. God chose us in Christ before the foundation of the world so we may be holy and blameless in His sight. Why? So that we may praise Him for His glorious grace that has been given to us in Jesus Christ! God alone deserves all the glory for our salvation.

In what ways does the doctrine of election show us God's glory and His grace?

In what ways have you been reminded of the bigness of God and His massive, redemptive story?

GROUP STUDY

Warm Up

Take a moment to read these quotes about election and predestination from the world of church history and leadership. Each quote sheds light on a different view or angle from which we can learn. For the purpose of this group time, it isn't about one idea trumping the other. Instead, allow these different understandings of election and predestination to complement one another. Charles Spurgeon, a famous preacher in the 19th century, was once asked how he reconciled predestination with free will. Spurgeon just looked at the person who asked him the question and calmly said, "I do not try to reconcile friends."[4] Let that sink in as you begin your discussion.

In predetermining how salvation would be accomplished, the primary object of predestination was Jesus Christ himself. But in order to bring his saving work to pass, it was necessary for God secondarily to foreordain all the essential means of accomplishing this.[5]

JACK W. COTTRELL, THE FOREKNOWLEDGE VIEW

God predestines all events, yet not in such a way that violates genuine human freedom and choice. God meticulously "sets the table" so that humans freely choose what He had predetermined.[6]

KENNETH KEATHLEY, THE MIDDLE-KNOWLEDGE VIEW

Election refers to God's choosing whom to save. It is unconditional in that there is no condition man must meet before God chooses to save him. Man is dead in trespasses and sins. So there is no condition he can meet before God chooses to save him from his deadness.[7]

JOHN PIPER, THE UNCONDITIONAL VIEW

In what ways have you attempted to understand this biblical truth in the past? Did you lean more towards avoiding or embracing it?

Which notion helps you understand the doctrine of election in a way that is helpful and meaningful to your calling?

Discussion

First John 3:1 states, "Look at how great a love the Father has given us that we should be called God's children. And we are!" There it is. How great a love the Father has given! We can love God, go to church, put money in the offering plate, and help serve in different ministries, but that doesn't earn us any kind of right standing with God. Nothing we do can make us a good person before God. The Father has given us a great love; the Father has called us His children. The best thing we can do is recognize it for what it is, and praise Him in return.

During this time you'll have an opportunity to discuss what God revealed to you during the week. Listed below are some of the questions from your daily reading assignments. They will guide your small-group discussion.

1. Describe a time in your life when you gained a bigger vision or larger view of something important. In what ways did that change your attitude, emotions, and behavior?

2. How does it feel to be picked for something? How do you respond to this biblical truth that God picked you in Christ to be holy and blameless?

3. How does God's choosing you in Christ before the foundation of the world encourage you to live a holy and blameless life in God's sight?

4. How are you affected by the truth that your salvation is not an accident but the result of God's plan?

5. What are some specific actions that would reflect the blessing of your adoption through Christ into God's family?

6. What are some examples of spiritual blessings we receive from Christ? How do these spiritual blessings encourage you to praise God?

7. In what ways does the doctrine of election show us God's glory and His grace?

8. In what ways have you been reminded of the bigness of God and His massive, redemptive story?

Conclusion

Grasping the doctrine of election biblically—recognizing the work God has done since before time began to bring about your salvation and sanctification—will enlarge your vision of the greatness of our God. This will help you understand who you are in Christ. This will help you understand the depth of God's love on display in your salvation. This will help you praise the One who held back nothing to make you His child. God chose us in Him before the foundation of the world, and He calls us to respond and to believe.

Spend some time praying this for you and for your group:

"God, teach us how to live by this truth in a way that keeps us humble. Help us recognize Your sovereign plan as You open doors for us to build relationships with the lost. Thank You, God, for inviting us to share in Your mission for reaching the world with the gospel. Amen."

1. Gerald L. Bray, ed. *Galatians, Ephesians*, Reformation Commentary on Scripture (Downers Grove, IL: InterVarsity Press, 2011), 245.
2. J.I Packer, "Introductory Message," in *The Death of Death in the Death of Christ* by John Owen (London: Banner of Truth, 1959), 4-5.
3. Adrian Rogers, *What Every Christian Ought to Know* (Nashville: B&H, 2005), 59-60.
4. Quoted in Lewis A. Drummond, *Theologians of the Baptist Tradition* (Nashville: B&H, 2001), 122.
5. Jack W. Cottrell, *Perspectives on Election* (Nashville: B&H, 2006), 115.
6. Kenneth Keathley, *Calvinism: A Southern Baptist Dialogue* (Nashville: B&H, 2008), 208.
7. John Piper, "What We Believe About the Five Points of Calvinism," *Desiring God*, March 1998, Accessed June 18, 2014, *http://www.desiringgod.org/articles/what-we-believe-about-the-five-points-of-calvinism*
8. Quoted in Thomas C. Oden and Mark J. Edwards, eds., *Galatians, Ephesians, Philippians*, Ancient Christian Commentary on Scripture (Downers Grove, IL: InterVarsity Press, 1999), 113.

> So that our love for him may become more fervent, he desires nothing from us except our salvation. He does not need our service or anything else but does everything for this end. One who openly expresses praise and wonder at God's grace will be more eager and zealous.[8]
>
> JOHN CHRYSOSTOM

NOTES

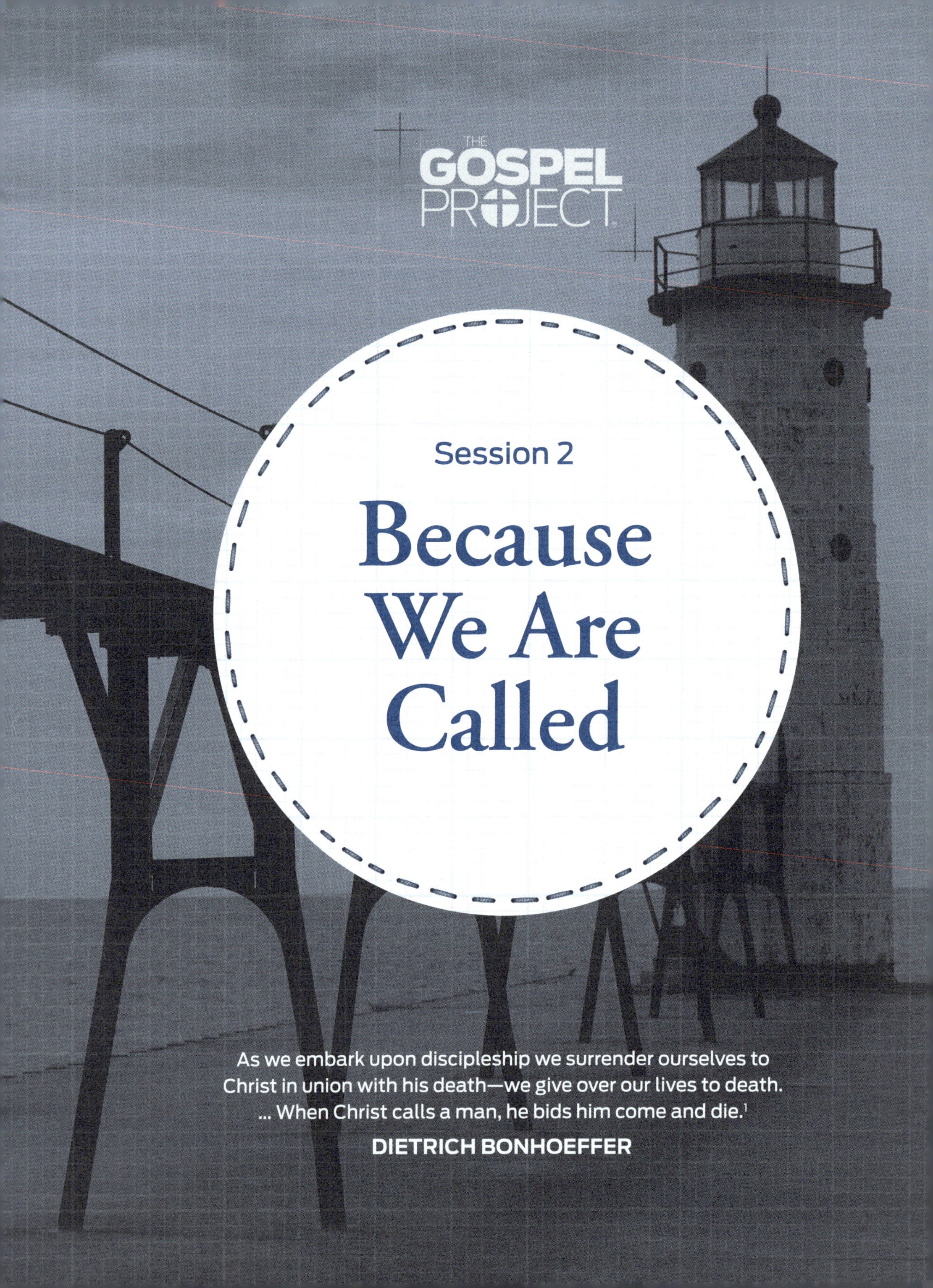

THE GOSPEL PROJECT

Session 2

Because We Are Called

As we embark upon discipleship we surrender ourselves to Christ in union with his death—we give over our lives to death. ... When Christ calls a man, he bids him come and die.[1]

DIETRICH BONHOEFFER

INDIVIDUAL STUDY

A teenage boy stood before a judge, charged again with breaking and entering and theft. Though still a juvenile, he was a menace to society. He had been kicked out of his home, and he provided for himself by selling valuable items he stole from others.

Surprisingly, the judge looked on the boy's plight and felt compassion. The judge had just buried his own 25-year-old son a month earlier after he succumbed to cancer. Instead of sentencing this criminal to juvenile detention, the judge offered to pay the penalty imposed on the boy and then made arrangements to adopt the boy as his own.

After several months, the boy asked the judge why he was showing so much love toward him. The judge explained, "This was the last will and testament of my only son. Before he died, he told me to find the most unworthy person I could and adopt him. You see, my son was loved every day of his life, and his death provided an opportunity for me to adopt you. You are now my son, my only son, and I will love you as I loved him."

What "last will and testament" stories—real or fiction—stand out to you? Explain.

The Second Epistle (Letter) to Timothy can be viewed as a sort of "last will and testament" of the apostle Paul, written during Paul's second imprisonment, shortly before his death. Paul was zealous and hopeful that Timothy would remember his holy calling and the glory of the gospel. He knew that if Timothy didn't remember these things, he might fall into temptation and desert the truth of the gospel.

In this lesson, we're going to explore Timothy's calling (and ours) to salvation and service. Those who've been called by God should exhibit humility in their salvation and confidence in their mission. God's grace in our salvation is the ultimate expression of God's love and mercy toward an undeserving people; this leads to our humility. In light of God's grace, Christians are to serve others in a variety of ways, heralding the good news of Jesus and calling others to submit to His lordship.

Throughout the week engage these daily study sections on your own. Each of these examines what it means to be called by God. There are three daily readings to prepare you before your group meets for this session. Interact with the Scriptures, and be ready to interact with your small group.

1 God Has Called Us to Salvation

[8] So don't be ashamed of the testimony about our Lord, or of me His prisoner. Instead, share in suffering for the gospel, relying on the power of God.
[9] He has saved us and called us with a holy calling, not according to our works, but according to His own purpose and grace, which was given to us in Christ Jesus before time began.
[10] This has now been made evident through the appearing of our Savior Christ Jesus, who has abolished death and has brought life and immortality to light through the gospel.

2 TIMOTHY 1:8-10

When asked what the point of life is, many people would say, "He who gets the most toys wins." Or, "Just try to be a good person and everything will work out okay." Or maybe even, "Believe whatever you want, but don't force your views on other people." None of these philosophies, however, line up with the worldview presented by the gospel. The gospel tells us that we made a mess, and Jesus cleaned it up. The world has been wrecked by sin and death through the sinful choices of people, yet Jesus made all things new through His life, death, and resurrection.

Believing this countercultural good news can be difficult. Sometimes we're tempted to believe the world's philosophies are correct and the Bible's words are incorrect. It's especially tempting when we're experiencing unexplainable suffering in our lives.

In verse 8, however, the apostle Paul reminded Timothy to not be ashamed of the gospel but to instead remember its power. This echoes what Paul said in Romans: "For I am not ashamed of the gospel, because it is God's power for salvation to everyone who believes, first to the Jew, and also to the Greek" (Rom. 1:16).

Paul was willing to suffer for the advancement of the gospel. After meeting Jesus, he dedicated his entire life to telling others the good news. Now, near the end of his life, he didn't want Timothy to lose faith. He was concerned that Timothy might see his suffering and decide the gospel wasn't worth it. So Paul reminded Timothy in his final letter to not be afraid and remember the gospel's power. Essentially, Paul was telling Timothy, "Believe what you know to be true, not just what your eyes see at this moment!"

What has caused you to be ashamed of the message of the gospel at times?

How have you seen the gospel work in your life or in the lives of others?

Paul encouraged Timothy to remember the gospel's power, and then he rehearsed the gospel message itself. He reminded Timothy what happened to him when he was saved. In verses 9-10, Paul put into words what happens to every believer when he or she comes to know Jesus—God saves them from darkness and calls them to realize a completely new identity as one in Christ.

Paul essentially told Timothy, "You didn't save yourself; God saved you! You didn't come to God yourself; God called you!" And Paul explained this wasn't because of what Timothy had done but according to God's own purpose and grace. The thing that makes the gospel utterly different from every other religion in the world is that it's based not on what we do for God but on what God has done for us. We offer nothing toward our salvation because God paid it in full through Christ. We need to see the truth that Jesus has accomplished fully what we couldn't do for ourselves, and He offers this grace to us freely according to His plan set out "before time began."

Under what circumstances and through whom did God call you to Himself?

If you buy collectibles of any type, then you know the importance of having a certificate of authenticity. Christianity has a certificate of authenticity to prove that the message of salvation is legitimate. Paul said that our salvation and calling are real, and the certificate of authenticity is found in the gospel—the life, death, and resurrection of Jesus. His death bought our life, and His resurrection certified the authenticity of this new life. Jesus lived the perfect life that we couldn't live. He died the death that we deserved to die. He rose again from the dead with power that we don't possess. These are real events that actually happened within history. No other religion claims such things. The life, death, and resurrection of Jesus prove that God really can accomplish what He calls us to—He can and will save us. Paul reminded Timothy of all these things to stir up his faith and to encourage him.

How does the "authentic" message of the gospel—Jesus' life, death, and resurrection—stir up your faith and encourage you?

2 God Has Called Us to Service

[11] For this gospel I was appointed a herald, apostle, and teacher,
[12] and that is why I suffer these things. But I am not ashamed, because
I know the One I have believed in and am persuaded that He is
able to guard what has been entrusted to me until that day.
2 TIMOTHY 1:11-12

How would you describe the essence of the Christian life? If you looked at a wide array of churches, you might come up with several competing ideas. You might assume it's all about worship music, sermons, big buildings, writing books, abstaining from sin, caring for the poor, or blogging. But how does the Bible describe the essence of Christianity? Paul would likely say that the essence of the Christian life is mission. Everyone who is saved by Jesus Christ is called to be on mission with Jesus Christ and for Jesus Christ.

Paul understood his calling in a three-fold manner—as a herald, apostle, and teacher.

1. A herald is someone who proclaims or preaches a message. So Paul was appointed to proclaim the message of the gospel.
2. The word *apostle* means "sent one." The apostles were Jesus' official representatives commissioned to take the message of the gospel into the whole world. So Paul was appointed to go and spread the good news of the risen Savior.
3. Finally, Paul said he was appointed to be a teacher. Paul was appointed to teach and explain the gospel and its implications to the people to whom he was sent.

Though Paul was referring to his own specific calling in verse 11, the calling of every believer is essentially the same—first to salvation and also to service. The majority of Christians aren't called to be preachers in the sense of vocationally pastoring a church, but all Christians are called to be people who proclaim the good news of the King. Our identity in Christ is a missionary identity.

God doesn't save us just to sit and watch the Sunday show while calling it church. God saves us from something (sin), to Someone (God), and for something (mission). God saves us from sin and for mission based on our new identity as a child of God; therefore, we take on the nature of our missionary God. Mission is who we are, and it's also what we do. When God saved you, He saved you for a purpose. The purpose of salvation is that each believer might produce a life of obedience and holiness to God instead of self. Believers are sent into the world for good works (see Eph. 2:8-10), and the primary good work that all believers are called to participate in is the work of showing and sharing the love of Jesus to the entire world, especially those who don't know Him.

How would you describe your calling through the gospel to service and mission? To what degree do you understand your being sent?

How can we discern our calling to service? Believers are called not only to a life of mission but also to use specific gifts that God places in our lives. The apostle Paul was given a specific appointment and the necessary gifts; God made him a herald, apostle, and teacher. Likewise, everyone who is in Christ has a specific appointment and gifting. We're all called to mission, but not exactly in the same way. Your appointment and gifting will not be the same as the apostle Paul's, nor anyone else's for that matter. It will be unique to you (see 1 Cor. 12).

So what is your gift? The Bible gives some different lists of various spiritual gifts (see Rom. 12:6-8; 1 Cor. 12:4-11; Eph. 4:11-12; 1 Pet. 4:9-11). These lists are probably not exhaustive since they don't line up exactly. Many pastors encourage their congregation to take a "spiritual gifts inventory" as a tool to help figure out their gifting from God. These inventories should be seen as a launching point for the Holy Spirit to reveal His gifts to you. Subsequently, your gifts will be confirmed by those in the church who know you best.

Sometimes the best way to discern your spiritual gift is to start serving in the church. While you use your gifts, you can serve one another in the church. Or you can join with other believers to serve hurting people through your church. Finally, you may be called to use your gifts as you are sent out to minister beyond your church's organized ministries.

How do you think God has gifted you to give glory to Him in your service to others? What has been your experience so far?

One note of caution: Please don't confuse the command that Jesus gives all of us to be on mission with your unique spiritual gifting. God may have gifted you to be an encourager, but your gift of encouragement doesn't exempt you from a calling to share the gospel. Rather, our spiritual gifts and our call to proclaim the gospel will work hand in hand. Your God-bestowed gift to encourage others will likely lead to opportunities to share the gospel more effectively.

What are some dangers of working and operating outside our giftedness for long periods of time? In what ways are Christians tempted to outwork God?

3 God Has Called Us to Submission

[13] Hold on to the pattern of sound teaching that you have heard from me, in the faith and love that are in Christ Jesus. [14] Guard, through the Holy Spirit who lives in us, that good thing entrusted to you.
2 TIMOTHY 1:13-14

Finally, Paul instructed Timothy to hold tightly to the pattern of sound teaching that he heard from Paul. The idea Paul was seeking to convey through his words was the idea of a blueprint. Timothy was to remember the sound teaching that characterized Paul's ministry and to continue in that tradition. It's important to note that Paul didn't tell Timothy to hold tightly to the methods that he used but rather to hold tightly to the pattern of sound teaching that he received. In other words, Paul wasn't telling Timothy to do everything exactly the way that he did it. Timothy would have to chart his own ministry course. The thing that would remain constant, however, was the gospel message.

Jim Collins tells a story in his book *Good to Great* about a CEO who for years led his company by always trying to emulate the founder. What eventually became apparent to everyone was that this CEO wasn't leading the company in an efficient manner. He was trying to do everything that his mentor had done without any thought to how his company might perform best in the current situation. The results were not good.

In Christian ministry, the situation is similar. The context of ministry continually changes, and we must prayerfully consider how best to convey the message of the gospel and to obey the commands of Jesus in our own time and place. At the same time, we recognize that the gospel doesn't change. Like our Lord and Savior, the message is the same yesterday, today, and forever.

In order for Timothy to be a successful minister, Paul encouraged him to hold to the pattern of sound teaching, not to mimic Paul in everything that he did. His concern was for the message of the gospel:

[1] When I came to you, brothers, announcing the testimony of God to you, I did not come with brilliance of speech or wisdom. [2] For I didn't think it was a good idea to know anything among you except Jesus Christ and Him crucified.
1 CORINTHIANS 2:1-2

> But even if we or an angel from heaven should preach to you a gospel other than what we have preached to you, a curse be on him!
> GALATIANS 1:8

In what ways is the pattern of sound teaching—the gospel—threatened, both inside and outside the church?

This last point is really an expansion of the points that Paul has made. We must pay careful attention to the ministry that God has given us and guard it. At the same time, we must realize that we don't have the power to do this on our own. Paul instructed Timothy to "Guard through the Holy Spirit." In the face of suffering, persecution, imprisonment, and even death, the power to hold fast to the truth of the gospel lies in the Holy Spirit—the One who opened our ears to God's call and was given to us when we responded to it.

What evidence of the Holy Spirit's power to guard the gospel have you seen in your life?

How do we partner with the Holy Spirit to guard the ministry that has been entrusted to us?

> If we offer glory to God in the Spirit, we mean that the Spirit enables us to fulfill the requirements of true religion. According to this usage, then, we say we are in the Spirit, but it is not objectionable for someone to testify, 'the Spirit of God is in me, and I offer glory because his grace has given me the wisdom to do so.[2]
>
> **BASIL THE GREAT**

GROUP STUDY

Warm Up

The Bible consistently informs us that salvation is the work of God. Notice the saving work of God alone in these passages:

> [13] But Moses said to the people, "Don't be afraid. Stand firm and see the LORD's salvation He will provide for you today; for the Egyptians you see today, you will never see again. [14] The LORD will fight for you; you must be quiet."
>
> EXODUS 14:13-14

> A woman named Lydia, a dealer in purple cloth from the city of Thyatira, who worshiped God, was listening. The Lord opened her heart to pay attention to what was spoken by Paul.
>
> ACTS 16:14

> [15] But when God, who from my birth set me apart and called me by His grace, was pleased [16] to reveal His Son in me, so that I could preach Him among the Gentiles, I did not immediately consult with anyone.
>
> GALATIANS 1:15-16

In what ways do you notice the saving work of God in the passages above?

Think about your own salvation experience. How do you see God as the Source and Initiator of your faith journey with Him?

God is the Source of salvation, not people. God brought the Israelites out of Egypt and led them to the promised land by His mighty hand alone. Moses and the people couldn't do it. God opened the heart of Lydia; she didn't initiate her salvation. God set Paul apart from birth and called him. Paul didn't call himself; in fact, he was God's enemy. His ears were deaf to the call of God, but God was powerful enough to unstop the ears of Paul so he could hear the truth. And Jesus, through His life, death, and resurrection, accomplished the ultimate work of salvation that made all of this possible.

Discussion

When you think about it, God's saving work is contained within the gospel. In Romans 1:16-17, Paul said that the gospel reveals the righteousness of God, and within the gospel "it contains the power to save." This is why the gospel can't change. It doesn't need to be validated. It validates itself because it contains the power of God to save any and all who will hear and believe.

> The gospel was formulated by the apostles and has now been bequeathed by them to the church. It is found in its definitive form in the New Testament. This apostolic New Testament faith is regulative for the church of every age and place. The church is "built upon the foundation of the apostles and prophets" (Eph. 2:20). There is no other gospel. There can be no new gospel.[3]
>
> **JOHN STOTT**

During this time you will have an opportunity to discuss what God revealed to you during the week. Listed below are some of the questions from your daily reading assignments. They will guide your small-group discussion.

1. What ways are we tempted to be ashamed of the message of the gospel at times?

2. How have you seen the gospel work powerfully in your life or in the lives of others?

3. Under what circumstances and through whom did God call you to Himself?

4. How does the "authentic" message of the gospel—Jesus' life, death, and resurrection—stir up your faith and encourage you?

5. How would you describe your calling through the gospel to service and mission? To what degree do you understand your being sent?

6. How do you think God has gifted you to give glory to Him in your service to others? What has been your experience so far?

7. What are some dangers of working and operating outside our giftedness for long periods of time? In what ways are Christians tempted to outwork God?

Conclusion

God called Paul and Timothy and us to salvation and to service, and our response to this call will be reflected in our submission to the gospel of God's Word. Are we responding to the call in obedience to our mission to share this good news of Jesus' life, death, and resurrection on our behalf? Are we guarding—through the power of the Holy Spirit, in our words and our actions—the gospel call that rings out to all peoples, tribes, tongues, and nations? God has called. How will you respond?

Spend some time praying this for you and for your group:

> "God, we say 'thanks' and rejoice that You have called us out of sin and into salvation. Help us to take steps of obedience in responding to Your calling in Christ. Bring us into complete submission to Your Word and Your will. Amen."

1. Dietrich Bonhoeffer, *The Cost of Discipleship* (New York: Touchstone, 1995), 89.
2. Saint Basil, *On The Holy Spirit* (Crestwood, NY: St. Vladimir's Seminary Press, 1980), 96.
3. John Stott, *The Message of 2 Timothy* (Downers Grove, IL: InterVarsity Press, 1973), 41.
4. Quoted in Philip Schaff, ed. *A Select Library of the Nicene and Post-Nicene Fathers of the Christian Church* (New York: The Christian Literature Company, 1889), 480.

> If then He is mighty in calling us, and good, in that He hath done it of grace and not of debt, we ought not to fear. For He Who, when we should have perished, saved us, though enemies, by grace, will He not much more co-operate with us, when He sees us working? 'Not according to our own works,' he says, 'but according to his own purpose and grace,' that is, no one compelling, no one counseling Him, but of His own purpose, from the impulse of His own goodness, He saved us; for this is the meaning of 'according to his own purpose.[4]
>
> JOHN CHRYSOSTOM

NOTES

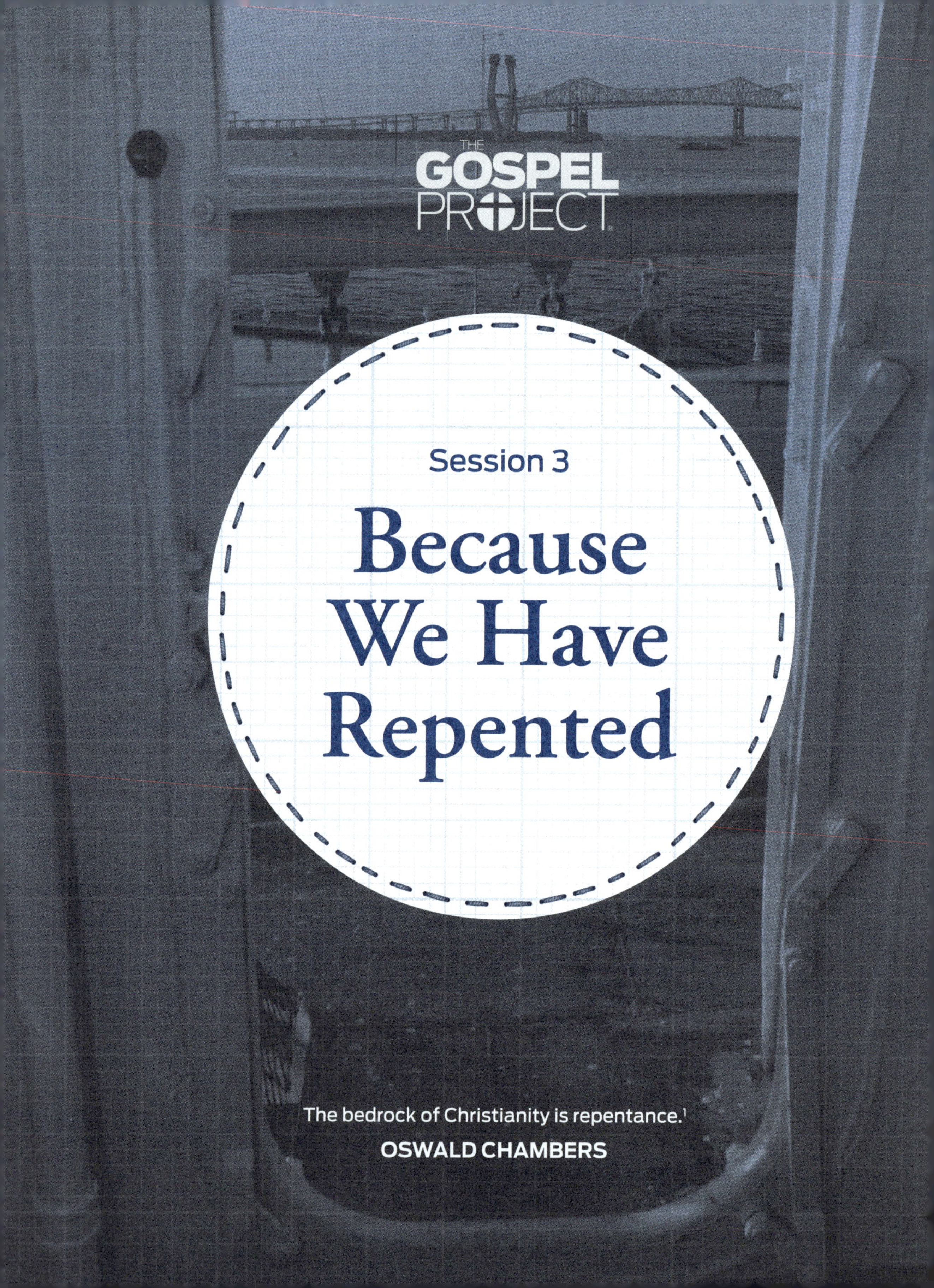

Session 3

Because We Have Repented

The bedrock of Christianity is repentance.[1]

OSWALD CHAMBERS

INDIVIDUAL STUDY

Are you a repenter?

Have you ever been asked that question? Have you ever thought to describe or label yourself in such a way? At some point in the last century, evangelicals in Romania received this derogatory label. They were called *repenters*. This word in Romanian described those who had, in fact, repented of sin, turned to Christ, and then sought to live in a state of repentance.

Rather than resist the label, the Romanian Christians embraced it. "That's exactly who we are," they said. They challenged everyone to avoid a life of nominal Christianity and instead live a life of repentance.

How would you define *repentance* in your own words?

Think of a time when you repented of something you were doing wrong. How long did it last?

When you think about it, that question sums up a distinctive attribute between Christ followers and the rest of the world. We repent. We believe in a conversion—a turning away from sin toward God in faith as a response to God's gracious initiative in calling us to salvation. Christianity hinges on repentance, a journey of putting to death our sins and living for the One who has saved us.

In this session, we'll look at the nature of true repentance. We'll see that repentance is a response to God's gracious call to salvation. We feel sorrow for our sin in light of God's goodness and mercy to us; we turn from our sin and embrace Jesus as our Savior and then strive to obey Jesus as our King. Repentance results in a changed life with a missional focus that leads us to call others to repentance.

Throughout the week engage these daily study sections on your own. Each examines what it means to repent. There are three daily readings to prepare you before your group meets for this session. Interact with the Scriptures, and be ready to interact with your small group.

1 Sorrow for Sin in Light of God's Goodness

There's a difference between true repentance and remorse. There are ways to make yourself feel bad about doing something, to manufacture a feeling of remorse. A child who comes home with a note from the teacher may feel bad because she'll have to endure the consequences of her actions. She may feel remorse for her behavior, but is that repentance?

The difference between remorse and repentance doesn't go away when we're adults. We may feel bad about the consequences of our sin—losing our temper, cheating at work, getting a speeding ticket. So shedding tears out of sorrow, remorseful and repentant may look the same on the outside. But the heart keeps the true record of repentance—and God sees the difference.

True repentance is sorrow for sin in light of God's goodness and power. We see an example of true repentance in the story of a fisherman, Simon Peter, who encountered the goodness and power of Jesus. He recognized his own sinfulness and worshiped the Savior.

> 1 As the crowd was pressing in on Jesus to hear God's word, He was standing
> by Lake Gennesaret. 2 He saw two boats at the edge of the lake; the fishermen
> had left them and were washing their nets. 3 He got into one of the boats, which
> belonged to Simon, and asked him to put out a little from the land. Then He
> sat down and was teaching the crowds from the boat. 4 When He had finished
> speaking, He said to Simon, "Put out into deep water and let down your nets
> for a catch." 5 "Master," Simon replied, "we've worked hard all night long and
> caught nothing! But at Your word, I'll let down the nets." 6 When they did this,
> they caught a great number of fish, and their nets began to tear. 7 So they
> signaled to their partners in the other boat to come and help them; they came
> and filled both boats so full that they began to sink. 8 When Simon Peter saw this,
> he fell at Jesus' knees and said, "Go away from me, because I'm a sinful man,
> Lord!" 9 For he and all those with him were amazed at the catch of fish they took,
> 10 and so were James and John, Zebedee's sons, who were Simon's partners.
> "Don't be afraid," Jesus told Simon. "From now on you will be catching people!"
> 11 Then they brought the boats to land, left everything, and followed Him.
>
> LUKE 5:1-11

Amazed at Jesus' power, Peter fell to his knees and confessed his sinfulness, and then he left everything behind to follow Christ. This is the evidence of true repentance. It's more than remorse or regret over the consequences of one's sin. There is sorrow, but it's grounded in the recognition that we're totally undeserving of salvation.

How would you describe the difference between remorse and repentance?

Remorse is the starting point of repentance, but it's not all repentance entails. Judas, for example, felt remorse after betraying Jesus, but his grief was worldly, leading to death by suicide. Peter, on the other hand, felt remorse after denying Christ, but his grief led to a life on mission for Christ.

Another sign of true repentance is that we feel sorrow for sin because of God's goodness, not just His judgment. In other words, repentance is a response of the heart to the grace of God. It's not driven merely by fear of punishment. Peter didn't repent because he was afraid of judgment; he repented because he had just witnessed a miraculous display of kindness. And it's God's kindness that leads us to repentance.

When we recognize how we deserve immediate death for our sins, we're stunned by the graciousness of a God who allows us to continue breathing, living, and going about in this world. It's not the fear of hell that leads us to repentance but the goodness of God to warn us against going there.

Why is it important that our repentance be a response to God's goodness, not just a fear of punishment?

True repentance is a response to God's power, not a work of our own power. For centuries, many Christians saw repentance as synonymous with "doing penance." The way to turn to God was to do good works in order to win His favor. But throughout Scripture, we see repentance as an inward change—to change your mind about something and let your outward actions follow with consistency.

What are some acts of penance people perform to earn their way toward God? What do these look like when placed beside the grace of God?

As we talk with non-Christians, it's important for us to speak of the Bible's warnings about judgment. How can we do so without leading people to repent merely out of fear?

2 Renounce Sin and Embrace the Savior

Repentance begins with remorse, but it quickly moves to a renouncing of sin and embracing the Savior. When the apostle Paul stood before King Agrippa and recounted his conversion experience, he made it clear that his mission was to call people to repent, to turn from one way of life to another. It's a change of mind and heart that leads to a changed life. Look carefully at how he described his task in calling people to repentance:

> 15 "Then I said, 'Who are You, Lord?'
> "And the Lord replied: 'I am Jesus, the One you are persecuting. 16 But get up and stand on your feet. For I have appeared to you for this purpose, to appoint you as a servant and a witness of what you have seen and of what I will reveal to you. 17 I will rescue you from the people and from the Gentiles. I now send you to them 18 to open their eyes so they may turn from darkness to light and from the power of Satan to God, that by faith in Me they may receive forgiveness of sins and a share among those who are sanctified.'
> 19 "Therefore, King Agrippa, I was not disobedient to the heavenly vision. 20 Instead, I preached to those in Damascus first, and to those in Jerusalem and in all the region of Judea, and to the Gentiles, that they should repent and turn to God, and do works worthy of repentance.
> ACTS 26:15-20

In fulfilling his commission to spread the gospel, Paul called for faith and repentance. Conversion is expressed in three ways in this passage: turning from darkness to light (v. 18), turning from the power of Satan to God (v. 18), and turning from sin to do works worthy of repentance (v. 20).

From Darkness to Light. Before we come to Christ, we are moving around this world in the dark, unable to see the beauty of Christ and unwilling to accept the light. But once we repent, we turn from darkness to light. We pursue the light, no longer content to stumble around in the dark. We have a purpose given to us by the Light of the world who has shone in our hearts.

From the Power of Satan to God. Second, note how Paul described this "turning" more personally than just light and darkness. He called people to turn from the power of Satan to God. We're switching kingdoms. Just as a person who is applying for citizenship in one country usually renounces their former citizenship, we pledge allegiance to King Jesus and renounce Satan and his power.

The early church asked of every adult who stepped into the baptismal waters: "Do you renounce Satan and all the spiritual forces of wickedness? Do you renounce the evil powers of this world which corrupt and destroy the creatures of God? Do you renounce all sinful desires that draw you from the love of God?" The baptismal candidate would answer "I renounce them" to each of these questions.[2]

Then the questions turned to the positive side of repentance: "Do you turn to Jesus Christ and accept Him as your Savior? Do you put your whole trust in His grace and love? Do you promise to follow and obey Him as your Lord?" And the candidate would respond, "I do," much like a wedding service.[3]

Why is it important for us to see repentance from both sides—turning from sin and turning to Christ?

From Sin to Works Worthy of Repentance. The last aspect of repentance that Paul mentioned in this chapter centers on turning to God and doing works worthy of repentance. The renunciation of sin isn't all that repentance entails. Turning to God implies we replace those evil deeds with good ones, with actions that are worthy of our new identity in Christ.

Don't misunderstand the phrase. The "worth" here doesn't refer to us earning favor with God or somehow becoming deserving of repentance. We don't deserve God's grace; that's why it's grace—unmerited favor. The works described here refer to living in light of our new identity. It implies that repentance is valuable, which means we should act in a way that showcases its value. All of our good deeds should showcase the worth of God and the beauty of the gospel.

What are some deeds that do not "fit" in a repentant person's life?

What are some ways we may seek to limit Christ's claim on our lives?

3 Moving Toward Purposeful Obedience

Imagine this scenario. You're sightseeing in a European city, walking down streets looking for a national landmark. You ask someone on the street where the landmark is and find out you're going the wrong way. At this point, you have a choice to make. You can continue on your path, assuming you know better than the local. Or you can turn around and go the other direction. But turning around involves taking steps in the new direction. It would be silly to take the advice of the local person, turn around, and then stand still. You would never reach the landmark simply by turning. You have to take steps in the other direction.

In considering the nature of repentance, we've focused on the turning around aspect. It's important for us to focus also on taking steps of obedience as a result of true repentance, a true "turning." We see this in the language of "turning" we find in the Old Testament.

> 57 The LORD is my portion; I have promised to keep Your words. 58 I have sought Your favor with all my heart; be gracious to me according to Your promise. 59 I thought about my ways and turned my steps back to Your decrees. 60 I hurried, not hesitating to keep Your commands.
>
> PSALM 119:57-60

The repentant sinner has a desire to keep God's Word. His obedience is purposeful, and there is a sense of urgency attached to it. Note how the psalmist, after turning his steps, hurries without hesitation to keep God's commands.

Repentance isn't something that comes naturally. We cultivate a life of ongoing repentance on purpose. We consider our actions in light of God's grace toward us through the cross and resurrection of Jesus Christ. Then we walk in a new way of life, committing daily to follow our Savior. We put to death the deeds of the flesh as we walk by the Spirit.

How can we encourage one another to repent regularly?

One of the primary ways we take steps of purposeful obedience is to join God in His mission. Earlier, we looked at the story of Peter's repentant spirit in response to Christ's miraculous display of power and grace. He felt sorrow for his sin and committed to following Christ. We should remember, however, how that story ended. His following Christ entailed fishing for people. He didn't simply renounce sin; he also received an evangelistic commission.

The same held true of the apostle Paul. We saw earlier how he recounted his conversion experience to King Agrippa. Note that Paul's repentance was expressed in his embrace of this new calling on his life: to summon others to turn from darkness to light.

The repentant person isn't content to step into the light and leave everyone else in the dark. We shouldn't be content with celebrating our freedom from Satan's tyranny while we dismiss the countless people around us still in chains. Repentance entails a life of mission. The purposeful obedience on display in our lives of ongoing repentance is a missional obedience. As we walk worthy of repentance, we call others to follow Jesus.

What is the connection between repentance and our mission as Christ's followers?

In what ways can Christ followers help the lost recognize their need to repent and find forgiveness in Christ?

GROUP STUDY

Warm Up

In Matthew 3:1-12, the story of John the Baptist is recorded. Think about the ministry of John the Baptist as a forerunner of the Messiah. His purpose was to prepare the way for Jesus. What was a definitive mark of his ministry? John baptized his disciples with a baptism of repentance. Read the following passage, and let it be the template for this conversation.

1 In those days John the Baptist came, preaching in the Wilderness of Judea
2 and saying, "Repent, because the kingdom of heaven has come near!"
3 For he is the one spoken of through the prophet Isaiah, who said:

A voice of one crying out in the wilderness:
Prepare the way for the Lord; make His paths straight!

4 John himself had a camel-hair garment with a leather belt around his waist, and
his food was locusts and wild honey. 5 Then people from Jerusalem, all Judea,
and all the vicinity of the Jordan were flocking to him, 6 and they were baptized by
him in the Jordan River as they confessed their sins. 7 When he saw many of the
Pharisees and Sadducees coming to the place of his baptism, he said to them,
"Brood of vipers! Who warned you to flee from the coming wrath? 8 Therefore
produce fruit consistent with repentance. 9 And don't presume to say to yourselves,
'We have Abraham as our father.' For I tell you that God is able to raise up children
for Abraham from these stones! 10 Even now the ax is ready to strike the root of
the trees! Therefore, every tree that doesn't produce good fruit will be cut down
and thrown into the fire. 11 "I baptize you with water for repentance, but the One
who is coming after me is more powerful than I. I am not worthy to remove His
sandals. He Himself will baptize you with the Holy Spirit and fire. 12 His winnowing
shovel is in His hand, and He will clear His threshing floor and gather His wheat
into the barn. But the chaff He will burn up with fire that never goes out."

What are the implications of John's ministry here? In what ways does repentance prepare the way for us to participate in God's kingdom?

Describe the condition of your heart before and after you repented. How did your view of Jesus change once you repented of sin?

Discussion

E. Y. Mullins states, "The first act of true repentance introduces the penitent into the Christian life. But this act is not a mere legal transaction which is over and done with once for all. It is a permanent moral process going on every day. Every renunciation of sin, every putting off of the old man, is in essence the repetition of the first act of repentance. Hence it is an attitude of the soul to be cultivated. The definite and positive renunciation of sin in every form should become the fixed habit of the soul."[4]

During this time you will have an opportunity to discuss what God revealed to you during the week, and how you can cultivate this "attitude of the soul." Listed below are some of the questions from your daily reading assignments. They will guide your small-group discussion.

1. How would you describe the difference between remorse and repentance?

2. Think of a time when you repented of something you were doing wrong. How long did it last?

3. Why is it important that our repentance be a response to God's goodness, not just a fear of punishment?

4. What are some acts of penance people perform to earn their way toward God? What do these acts look like when placed beside the marvelous grace of God?

5. Why is it important for us to see repentance from both sides—turning from sin and turning to Christ?

6. How can we encourage one another to repent regularly?

7. What is the connection between repentance and our mission as Christ's followers?

Conclusion

Though they were derided as repenters, Romanian believers understood that this label said something true about them. They embraced the label because they embraced the identity. They understood that the Christian life is one of repentance. No matter the intentions of those who would mock them, the term was accurate.

Christians turn from our sin (repentance) and turn to Christ for salvation (faith). Conversion involves both repentance and faith. Though we have examined the nature of repentance in this session, both repentance and faith are inseparable. Believers repent and repenters believe.

> Repentance involves a radical change of heart and mind in which we agree with God's evaluation of our sin and then take specific action to align ourselves with His will. ... The evidence of repentance is not words of resolve, but a changed life.[5]
>
> HENRY T. BLACKABY

Spend some time praying this for you and for your group:

"God, grant us true repentance that leads to good works. Help us see the need for personal repentance as we follow You on mission to reach others. Amen."

1. Oswald Chambers, "Repentance," *Daily Devotionals by Oswald Chambers*, December 7, 2013, Accessed June 18, 2014, *http://utmost.org/classic/repentance-classic/*.
2. Robert E. Webber, *Ancient-Future Time* (Grand Rapids: Baker, 2004) [eBook]
3. Ibid.
4. E.Y. Mullins, *The Christian Religion in Doctrinal Expression* (Roger Williams Press, 1917), 370.
5. Henry Blackaby, *Experiencing God Day-By-Day Devotional* (Nashville: B&H, 1998), 162.
6. J.I. Packer, *Evangelism and the Sovereignty of God* (Downers Grove, IL: InterVarsity Press, 2008), 81.

> The repentance that Christ requires of His people consists in a settled refusal to set any limits to the claims which He may make on their lives.[6]
>
> **J.I. PACKER**

NOTES

THE GOSPEL PROJECT

Session 4

Because We Believe

It is not great faith we need: it is faith in a great God.[1]

N.T. WRIGHT

INDIVIDUAL STUDY

Faith is popular nowadays. Look at the bestselling songs and you'll find a number of them telling you to "just believe," and never give up the faith you need to follow your dreams. Look at bestselling books that urge you to have faith in yourself, your abilities, and your future. You can achieve your goals in life—if you just believe in yourself! Look at movies where the main characters learn how to summon the energy to believe in their own abilities to reach their full potential and destiny.

Keep your eyes and ears open. You'll find people talking about "faith" or describing someone as "a person of faith." But what is true faith, and are we really talking about it? It does seems like the common use of the word *faith* in our culture is less about what we trust in and more about how much we accomplish. The object of faith seems irrelevant. All you need to do is just believe.

We're told that we'll do wonderful things if we just believe in ourselves. But we've all had times where we've truly believed—and completely failed. Did our faith fail? Did we do it wrong? Was our faith misplaced? Should we have had more faith in ourselves?

What do you think is usually meant by the term *person of faith*? How might this description vary from person to person?

Biblical faith isn't just about the person who believes. It's about the Person in whom we believe. It's not about having faith in a general sense but putting our trust in Someone who is actually worthy of our faith. The object of our faith is what matters. Put your faith in the wrong thing and it doesn't matter how much you believe. Biblical faith is about the believer and the "believed in."

In this session, we'll look at the nature of true faith. We'll see that biblical faith begins with a recognition and confession of our belief in the truthfulness of the gospel. Faith means we receive Christ personally as the Lord and Savior of our lives, and we rest upon Him alone for salvation. As children of God who live in the light, we're to express our faith through love for others.

Throughout the week engage these daily study sections on your own. Each of these examines what it means to put faith in God. There are three daily readings to prepare you before your group meets for this session. Interact with the Scriptures, and be ready to interact with your small group.

1 Recognizing the Truth of the Gospel

There are plenty of people in our society who believe in a God of some sort. Perhaps their view of God is close to the Bible's portrayal. Perhaps their view is different. Nevertheless, the majority of the world's population believes in a higher power, a divine being. Atheistic apologists may make a lot of noise, but most people go on believing God exists, even if they have wide-ranging views on what that God is like or how involved He is in our lives.

Christians also believe in the existence of God, but we're distinct from the world in what we affirm about this God who exists. Specifically speaking, we believe in the gospel—the good news about Jesus Christ and what He has done for us. We don't believe in a generic God or an impersonal force. We believe in God as He has revealed Himself—Father, Son, and Holy Spirit.

In the apostle John's letter near the end of the New Testament, we see how Christian faith is closely connected to particular truths about Jesus. To be a Christian is to recognize the truth of who Jesus is and what He has done.

> 13 This is how we know that we remain in Him and He in us: He has given
> assurance to us from His Spirit. 14 And we have seen and we testify that the
> Father has sent His Son as the world's Savior. 15 Whoever confesses that
> Jesus is the Son of God—God remains in him and he in God. 16 And we have
> come to know and to believe the love that God has for us. God is love, and
> the one who remains in love remains in God, and God remains in him.
> 1 JOHN 4:13-16

Notice the truths that a Christian must believe. We believe the message about Jesus—that the Father has sent His Son as the world's Savior (v. 14). This means we believe Jesus is the Messiah who saves us from sin.

Getting Jesus' identity right is essential to a biblical understanding of faith. Near the end of John's Gospel, we find this statement: "Jesus performed many other signs in the presence of His disciples that are not written in this book. But these are written so that you may believe Jesus is the Messiah, the Son of God, and by believing you may have life in His name" (John 20:30-31). John specified the purpose of His writing in no uncertain terms: "I want you to believe Jesus is the Messiah." In other words, believe the truth about Jesus' identity.

Jesus Himself warned about failing to get His identity right. In a heated confrontation with the Jewish leaders of His day, Jesus said, "If you do not believe that I am He, you will die in your sins" (John 8:24). This black-and-white statement of truth is difficult to square with our world's understanding of faith that says, "It doesn't matter what you believe, so long as you mean it." According to Jesus, believing the wrong thing about Him has eternal consequences.

Based on 1 John 4:13-16, what message are we called to believe?

Make a list of non-negotiable truths that a Christian must believe in order to be considered "Christian."

Why do these truths matter so much?

By faith, we recognize the truth of the gospel. We believe that Jesus is who He says He is. Closely connected to this message is the promise of God's love. Focus on verse 16 where it says we have come to know and believe God's love for us. At the heart of the gospel is God's love for humanity expressed through His saving work on our behalf. We experience this love and believe it's real. This isn't a fairy tale. We know this message is true.

What is the relationship between believing God loves you and experiencing His love for you?

Has there ever been a time when you believed in God's love for you but didn't sense it? How did you work through that trial of faith?

2 Receiving Christ as Savior and Lord

We've seen that biblical faith involves believing the message about Jesus. It involves believing certain propositions (such as, Jesus is the Messiah). But faith in the biblical sense doesn't stop with mere propositions. Those propositions carry us into the arms of a Person. One doesn't become a Christian only by assenting to biblical statements about Jesus. One becomes a Christian by receiving Christ personally as Savior and Lord.

We believe the Bible's message about Jesus is true. But even more than this, we believe in Jesus personally. We surrender our lives to Him as Savior and King. We can see how the message about Jesus and our personal faith in Jesus are connected by looking at part of the prologue to John's Gospel.

> 10 He was in the world, and the world was created through Him, yet the world did not recognize Him. 11 He came to His own, and His own people did not receive Him. 12 But to all who did receive Him, He gave them the right to be children of God, to those who believe in His name, 13 who were born, not of blood, or of the will of the flesh, or of the will of man, but of God.
> JOHN 1:10-13

There's a strong connection between recognizing the truth about Jesus and recognizing Jesus Himself. When Jesus came to His own people, they didn't receive Him. We see from the Gospel of John that when people failed to believe in Jesus' testimony about Himself, they also rejected Jesus personally. Failure to recognize the truth of the message leads to failure to receive Jesus.

On the flip side, however, the apostle John showed us what biblical faith looks like. It involves receiving Christ. This is much more than nodding your head at what the Bible says about Jesus. It's giving your heart to Him as Savior and King. It means receiving Christ into your life so that you'll be welcomed into the family of God and made His child.

What's the mark of those who are children of God? They believe in His name. Do you see how we've moved beyond receiving the message about Jesus to receiving Jesus Himself? Biblical faith is receiving Jesus as He is, not shaping Him into our image or making Him into someone else.

Why is it important to receive Christ personally? How does this add to your understanding of what it means to "live by faith"?

How would you explain the difference between merely assenting to the truth of the gospel and personally receiving Christ as Savior and Lord?

In the previous session, we looked at conversion through the angle of repentance. In this session, we're examining conversion through the angle of faith. It's important for us to remember that both of these go hand-in-hand. When we repent of our sins, we change directions and are transferred from one kingdom to another. When we put our faith in Christ, we move from darkness to light.

Why is it important not only to believe that Jesus is the Messiah, but also to believe in Jesus the Messiah?

3 Resting in Christ Alone for Salvation

Not only does true faith involve recognizing the truth of the gospel and receiving Christ as Savior and Lord, it also means we're to rest in Him alone for salvation. In other words, we don't put our trust in Jesus plus something else. It's Jesus alone who saves.

One of the most famous passages of Scripture reminds us of our need to believe in Jesus alone in order to escape judgment for our sins:

> 16 For God loved the world in this way: He gave His One and Only Son, so that
> everyone who believes in Him will not perish but have eternal life. 17 For God
> did not send His Son into the world that He might condemn the world, but
> that the world might be saved through Him. 18 Anyone who believes in Him
> is not condemned, but anyone who does not believe is already condemned,
> because he has not believed in the name of the One and Only Son of God.
> 19 "This, then, is the judgment: The light has come into the world, and people
> loved darkness rather than the light because their deeds were evil. 20 For
> everyone who practices wicked things hates the light and avoids it, so that
> his deeds may not be exposed. 21 But anyone who lives by the truth comes
> to the light, so that his works may be shown to be accomplished by God.
>
> JOHN 3:16-21

John 3:16 is the Bible's best-known verses. But let's look at its startling simplicity. It would be easy for people to rewrite end of verse 16 and add just a little bit of "works" to receive eternal life.

"So that everyone who believes in Him and lives a good life."
"So that everyone who believes in Him and gives generously to the poor."
"So that everyone who believes in Him and promises never to sin again will not perish."

No matter how hard we try or how far we drift, the Bible won't let us go there. Biblical faith is not about relying on Jesus as He is propped up by our good deeds. It's trusting in Him alone for salvation. It's personally putting our faith in Him. Why? Because that's the only way to escape judgment. The passage makes this clear in verses 17-19. Condemnation comes to those who do not believe in Christ. Only when we put our trust in the One and only Son of God are we able to join the family of God and be safe from the righteous judgment our sins deserve.

Why do you think trying to attain salvation through good deeds is offensive to God?

What do our efforts to achieve our own salvation say about Christ's sacrifice?

Once we recognize Jesus and place our faith in Him, we have a new life. It means we live in His light and leave behind the works of darkness. This is the point verses 19-21 make. Living by the truth means living in the light. We rest in Christ alone for salvation, and then we work, not to earn grace but as a response to grace. Resting in Christ leads us to living in His light, not the works of darkness (vv. 19-21), and pointing others to Christ.

In what ways does this passage's teaching on judgment provide urgency for our evangelistic efforts?

Resting in Christ also doesn't preclude seasons of doubt and difficulty in our lives. Some of the most well-known believers throughout church history passed through dark moments of despair and doubt. Tragedies strike and rock the foundation of our faith. At times, it seems like God is absent or distant, failing to listen to or respond to our prayers.

But even when our faith seems so small and ineffective, our God is mighty. Remember, it's not the size of your faith that matters most; it's the size of the Savior in whom we trust. Looking to Him and recalling the hope we have in things unseen (see Heb. 11:1), we can regain the confidence of biblical faith.

How does resting in Christ alone free us up to do the work He has called us to? Is it possible to be a faithful Christian and yet experience doubt and disillusionment?

GROUP STUDY

Warm Up

Many different things of this world can become "faith-killers." When Jesus walked the earth and pushed His disciples to believe, there were times when Jesus' frustration was seen. Four different times in four different situations, Jesus declared to His disciples, "O you of little faith!" Each time He made this declaration, Jesus revealed a different obstacle that was hindering their faith.

Worry

> If that's how God clothes the grass of the field, which is here today and thrown into the furnace tomorrow, won't He do much more for you—you of little faith?
>
> MATTHEW 6:30

Fear

> 25 So the disciples came and woke Him up, saying,
> "Lord, save us! We're going to die!"
> 26 But He said to them, "Why are you fearful, you of little faith?" Then He
> got up and rebuked the winds and the sea. And there was a great calm.
> 27 The men were amazed and asked, "What kind of man is
> this?—even the winds and the sea obey Him!"
>
> MATTHEW 8:25-27

Doubt

> Immediately Jesus reached out His hand, caught hold of him, and said to him, "You of little faith, why did you doubt?"
>
> MATTHEW 14:31

Reason

> Aware of this, Jesus said, "You of little faith! Why are you discussing among yourselves that you do not have bread?"
>
> MATTHEW 16:8

Which of the faith-killers above creep into your life?

What are other common obstacles that keep us from placing our faith in Christ?

Discussion

Tradition ascribes a story to Martin Luther during the Reformation. A church member came to him and said, "Pastor, why is it that week after week after week all you ever preach to us is the gospel?" The implication being that it was time to move onto some other topic. What was Luther's response?

"Well, because week after week you forget it."

Sometimes, it's good to just be reminded of what we've learned. When we remember the simple truths, we're more apt to stick to them. That's why we have group discussion. During this time you will have an opportunity to discuss what God revealed to you during the week. Listed below are some of the questions from your daily reading assignments. They will guide your small-group discussion.

1. What do you think is usually meant by the term "person of faith"? How might this description vary from person to person?

2. Make a list of non-negotiable truths that a Christian must believe in order to be considered "Christian." Why do these truths matter so much?

3. What is the relationship between believing God loves you and experiencing His love for you?

4. Why is it important to receive Christ personally? How does this add to your understanding of what it means to "live by faith"?

5. How would you explain the difference between merely assenting to the truth of the gospel and personally receiving Christ as Savior and Lord?

6. In what ways does this personal relationship with Christ impact our lives?

7. Why do you think trying to attain salvation through good deeds offensive to God?

8. How does resting in Christ alone free us up to do the work He has called us to? Is it possible to be a faithful Christian and yet experience doubt and disillusionment?

Conclusion

The Christian life demands not merely the acknowledgment of Christ's significance but our willingness to join Christ in carrying out His mission.[2]

CHARLES COLSON

Salvation comes through Jesus Christ alone, but our faith shows itself in our actions. The more we trust in Jesus, the more we become like Him. Growing in our faith means to grow in our resemblance to Him. This is why we're called to be on mission. The missionary Savior who gave His life for us is the One who calls us to give our lives for others, to join Him in His mission of changing lives. We spread the good news by proclaiming the events at the heart of our faith, by calling people to receive Christ as Savior and Lord, and by resting in Him alone for salvation.

Spend some time praying this for you and for your group:

"God, constantly remind us of the truths of the gospel that bring us back to our faith in You. Show us how to live a simple faith in front of those who need to see it. Use us so we can be children of light, and let us bring hope to this dark and dying world. Amen."

1. N.T. Wright, *Small Faith—Great God* (Downers Grove, IL: InterVarsity Press, 2010), 38.
2. Charles Colson, *The Faith* (Grand Rapids: Zondervan, 2008), 62.
3. Adrian Rogers, *Adrianisms*, vol. 2 (Memphis: Love Worth Finding Ministries, 2007), 186.

> Faith in faith is just positive thinking, but faith in Jesus is salvation.[3]
>
> **ADRIAN ROGERS**

NOTES

Session 5

Because We Are United

To be called into Christ is to be called into his mission (John 17:18). The call to conversion, the call to discipleship, the call to declare his wonderful deeds is the call to mission.[1]

FRANCIS DUBOSE

INDIVIDUAL STUDY

Gardening is more than just pulling weeds and planting perennials. Those who possess the "green thumb" understand more fully the complexities of seasons, climate, nature cycles, etc.

Consider, for instance, the time, energy, and expertise a gardener will spend maintaining a beautiful rose garden. The gardener will take care of all the plants—watering just the right amount, providing enough shade and pruning so they can come to full blossom. Year after year, the roses bloom to fruition, but that doesn't happen by coincidence. There is some meticulous manicuring happening on a daily basis. Whoever is tending the garden cares enough to intentionally prune the branches. Cutting away is essential for a thriving garden.

When you think about it, it does seem counterproductive. But taking a knife to a rosebush is the way you keep it healthy. You would think it would be the opposite—to shelter it, cover it up, and preserve it. But if we see the big picture, it makes sense for the rose garden to get that kind of attention, pruning, and care.

> Think about the things that will stop or hinder a plant from growing. How do all of these things work together to make a plant healthy and flourishing?

We need God's loving discipline in our lives if we're to grow up into spiritual health. God sees the big picture of our lives. The good news is that this discipline isn't cold and impersonal. It's rooted in the unity we share with Jesus Christ. This is essential to our spiritual growth. This is how we bear fruit, and how we display the love of God to others.

In this session, we'll look at the truth of our union with Christ—the central doctrine that sums up the reality of our salvation. When God saves us, we're united to His Son in order to bear good fruit, remain in His love, and fulfill our joy in Him. Christ is in us, and we're in Him. United to Christ, we're empowered to show the love of God to the world.

Throughout the week engage these daily study sections on your own. Each of these examines what it means to be united in Christ. There are three daily readings to prepare you before your group meets for this session. Interact with the Scriptures, and be ready to interact with your small group.

1 United to Christ, We Bear Good Fruit

[1] I am the true vine, and My Father is the vineyard keeper. [2] Every branch
in Me that does not produce fruit He removes, and He prunes every
branch that produces fruit so that it will produce more fruit. [3] You are
already clean because of the word I have spoken to you. [4] Remain in Me,
and I in you. Just as a branch is unable to produce fruit by itself unless
it remains on the vine, so neither can you unless you remain in Me.
[5] I am the vine; you are the branches. The one who remains in Me and
I in him produces much fruit, because you can do nothing without Me.
[6] If anyone does not remain in Me, he is thrown aside like a branch
and he withers. They gather them, throw them into the fire, and they
are burned. [7] If you remain in Me and My words remain in you, ask
whatever you want and it will be done for you. [8] My Father is glorified
by this: that you produce much fruit and prove to be My disciples.

JOHN 15:1-8

During His earthly ministry, Jesus said some stunning things. He claimed to be the Living Water that will satisfy human thirst. He claimed to be the Good Shepherd who takes care of His sheep. He said He was the Bread from heaven, and unless you eat His flesh and drink His blood, you will perish (He lost followers after that sermon!).

On the night He was betrayed, Jesus invested a well-known, Old Testament metaphor with new significance. He claimed to be the "true vine."

In the Old Testament, Israel was portrayed as the "vine" or "vineyard" of God (see Jer. 2:21, Isa. 5:1-7). Here were God's chosen people, tasked with bearing good fruit before the world so that all the nations would know the one true God. But Israel as "the vine" didn't blossom the way in which they were originally intended. How could God keep His promise to bless the whole world through Abraham's family if the family was failing to bear fruit?

When you look at a tree from a distance, you usually see the leaves and branches first. As you get closer to the base of the tree, you can look up and see how all the branches are connected organically to the trunk and how the leaves are connected organically to the branches. When winter comes and the leaves fall away, you can see every stem, every branch.

There's an organic unity to the trunk of a tree and its branches. In the same way, there is a unity between Jesus and His people. Notice that in this passage, Jesus tells us to remain in Him as He remains in us (see v. 4). Both of these aspects are true when we're united to Christ. Just as the branches remain on the vine in order to stay alive, so also must the life from the vine flow through all the branches.

Being united to Christ means we are in Him and He is in us. There's an organic unity to who we are in Christ. This truth goes to the heart of our identity as believers in Jesus. There are two sides to the one truth: we're "in Christ" and Christ is "in us."

Are you more likely to think of yourself as being "in Christ" or Christ being "in you"? Why do you think it's important to believe both parts of this important truth?

Think about this for a moment. We can do nothing apart from Jesus Christ. Nothing. We're like a flashlight with no batteries, like a TV unplugged from any power source, like a cell phone with no service. You get the picture.

So, we've seen that we can do nothing without Jesus, and God desires that our union in Christ produce fruit.But if we're producing fruit, then we're being pruned. God prunes the branches in our lives so that we'll bear even more fruit. Some people think that whenever we're in difficult circumstances, we must be doing something wrong, as if trials are a punishment for failing to bear good fruit. According to this passage, God prunes the branches that are fruitful.

What is the goal of our bearing fruit? What are some possible examples of God's "pruning" work in a person's life?

What are some ways you can encourage someone going through a difficult season when they feel like God is "punishing them"?

2 United to Christ, We Remain in God's Love

Jesus continued the discussion with His disciples by emphasizing the importance of living in His love. Notice how Christ proved His love to the Father. He obeyed Him, even if it meant dying on the cross.

> [9] As the Father has loved Me, I have also loved you. Remain in My love. [10] If you keep My commands you will remain in My love, just as I have kept My Father's commands and remain in His love.
>
> JOHN 15:9-10

There's no such thing as a loveless Christian. By definition, a believer in Jesus Christ is a believer in love. We're covered in God's love expressed through the sending of Jesus to die for us. God's love is expressed through Christ's life, death, resurrection, ascension, and promised return. We enter the realm of the Father's love for the Son as we bask in the Son's love for us (see v. 9).

The great tragedy of our day is this: many churches aren't known for the love their members share. *Loving* and *Christian* are not always descriptions that go together. This sad reality is a sign that we're failing to keep the Father's commands. In this passage, Jesus made it clear that the way we show we're in the love of Christ is by keeping the Father's commands the way Jesus did.

How can we tell if our church body is known for our love for one another?

How does one become an "unloving person"? In your opinion, what does a lack of love ultimately signify in a person's heart?

Remaining in God's love has eternal significance. As branches united to the true vine, we don't have to fear death. When we die, we die "in Christ," as several passages make clear. Paul wrote that "if we live, we live for the Lord; and if we die, we die for the Lord." Then he concluded, "Therefore, whether we live or die, we belong to the Lord" (Rom. 14:8). What a promise! The life of faith that began when we repented of our sins and trusted in Christ will continue beyond this life, all because we belong to the Lord!

Remaining in God's love isn't something we experience only here and now. When we die, we continue to be "in Christ." Our status doesn't change. For this reason, in another passage, Paul wrote about Christ's return and described Christians who have died as "the dead in Christ" (1 Thess. 4:16).

Christians don't just "die." We die "in Christ." As the last book of the Bible says, "The dead who die in the Lord from now on are blessed" (Rev. 14:13). In other words, the blessings of the Lord don't cease coming when we cease breathing. We die "in the Lord." The death of a Christian is fundamentally different than the death of an unbeliever because our death is "in Christ." What's more, our resurrection will be "in Christ" (Col. 3:11).

Remaining in God's love gives us hope for eternity. When we pass through the darkness of death, we have hope because we're united to the Light of the world who has gone before us—through death and out the other side in life. United to the resurrected One, we're assured of life beyond the grave, life that will last forever, for love is stronger than death.

In what ways does our assurance of God's love for us give us hope in the face of death?

How does knowing Christ's love for you give you strength to keep on loving others? Even those who don't deserve it?

3 United to Christ, Our Joy is Complete

There is another aspect of being united to Christ that we dare not miss: Christ's joy is shared with us. Most of the time, we don't think of Jesus as being joyful. Reading through the Gospels, we get a sense of His majesty, His humble spirit, His sadness at the grave of a friend, and His anger when confronted with religious hypocrisy. We see Him weeping for His unrepentant people as He is about to enter Jerusalem or healing the blind, the lame, and the leper. But Jesus also spoke about His great joy—the same joy He shares with us.

> 11 I have spoken these things to you so that My joy may be in you and your joy may
> be complete. 12 This is My command: Love one another as I have loved you.
> 13 No one has greater love than this, that someone would lay down his life for his
> friends. 14 You are My friends if you do what I command you. 15 I do not call you slaves
> anymore, because a slave doesn't know what his master is doing. I have called you
> friends, because I have made known to you everything I have heard from My Father.
> 16 You did not choose Me, but I chose you. I appointed you that you should go out
> and produce fruit and that your fruit should remain, so that whatever you ask the
> Father in My name, He will give you. 17 This is what I command you: Love one another.
>
> JOHN 15:11-17

Not only do we bear good fruit and remain in God's love, we find that our joy is made complete as we're united to Christ. There are all sorts of truths that increase our joy. One of them is friendship with God. Because of Christ's laying down His life for sinful human beings, we're able to become God's friends. We go from being enemies of God to being friends of God!

There's also joy in knowing we've been forgiven. The greatest love of all isn't "learning to love yourself," as some pop songs declare, but in laying down your life for friends. There's great joy in knowing the One who gave His life for us. Likewise, there's great joy in laying down our own lives for Him and for others. There's joy in being loved; there's joy in loving.

What's been the biggest obstacle for you in finding complete joy in Christ?

To what degree does your view of God's love help or hinder your ability to find true joy?

Jesus wants our joy to be complete, and the way our joy will be complete is when His joy is in us (v. 11). What was the source of Christ's joy? His relationship to the Father and His utter obedience to His will. The author of Hebrews said it was "for the joy that lay before Him" (Heb. 12:2) that Jesus endured the cross. Jesus' joy was formed by His mission to seek and save the lost.

God doesn't want dutiful Christians who see life as a drudgery of compliance. He desires that the same joy that flooded the heart of Christ, as He fulfilled His Father's will, would flood our hearts until we obey out of delight, not duty.

Missional obedience shouldn't be a begrudging acceptance of God's will and an obligatory fulfillment of God's commands. We're not "clock-punchers" in a factory, and God isn't the befuddled, agitated supervisor looking down on the warehouse. Begrudging evangelism inspires no one. United to Christ, our joy is made complete in fruitful obedience, love for God and neighbor, and friendship with God.

What is the connection between remaining in God and finding joy in God? Why do you believe both are necessary?

On a scale of 1 to 10, to what degree are you joyfully fulfilling your call to mission this week? Explain.

Why are you called a Christian? Because by faith I am a member of Christ and so I share in his anointing. I am anointed to confess his name, to present myself to him as a living sacrifice of thanks, to strive with a good conscience against sin and the devil in this life, and afterward to reign with Christ over all creation for all eternity.[2]

HEIDELBERG CATECHISM

GROUP STUDY

Warm Up

There are many implications of this teaching that we're united to Christ. Read the short list of implications below, and then answer the questions to begin your group time. Focus on the mission we have in Christ.

- We're united to Christ in His death.
- We're united to Christ in His resurrection.
- We're united to Christ as we represent Him to the world.
- We're united to Christ in His mission to seek and save the lost.
- We're united to Christ in knowing Him personally.

Describe how the Spirit (who raised Jesus from the dead) works powerfully in you. In what ways do you rely upon the Spirit's power to proclaim the gospel?

Describe how you die to yourself. What does that look like for you?

How are we connected to one another as we find ourselves united in Christ?

Discussion

Richard Longenecker states, "Being 'in Christ' is the essence of Christian proclamation and experience."[3] If we neglect this, if we live our lives without "treating the 'in Christ' motif, we miss the heart of the Christian message."[4] Take some time now to treat this "motif" in a thoughtful and prayerful manner.

Discuss with the group what God has revealed to you during the week. Listed below are some of the questions from your daily reading assignments. They will guide your small-group discussion.

1. Are you more likely to think of yourself as being "in Christ" or Christ being "in you"? Why do you think it's important to believe both parts of this important truth?

2. What is the goal of our bearing fruit? What are some possible examples of God's "pruning" work in a person's life?

3. What are some ways you can encourage someone going through a difficult season when they feel like God is "punishing them"?

4. How does one become an "unloving person"? In your opinion, what does a lack of love ultimately signify in a person's heart?

5. How does knowing Christ's love for you give you strength to keep on loving others? Even those who don't deserve it?

6. What's been the biggest obstacle for you in finding complete joy in Christ? To what degree does your view of God's love help or hinder your ability to find true joy?

7. On a scale of 1 to 10, to what degree are you joyfully fulfilling your call to mission this week? Explain.

Conclusion

We're saved because we're united in Christ—not just in this life, but in death and in the life to come.

> God declares that whatever our representative, the Lord Jesus Christ, has accomplished, those who trust in him have also achieved. His riches, righteousness, and merit belong to all who are in him (Rom. 8:17). Our union with Christ in his life, death, and resurrection provides the basis of our justification, sanctification, and glorification. From a historical perspective, our salvation is a finished feat, accomplished by Jesus of Nazareth nearly two thousand years ago.[5]
>
> KENNETH KEATHLEY

Spend some time praying this for you and for your group:

"God, give us a constant awareness that we can do nothing unless we are connected to Jesus. Keep us grounded in the truth that we are loved by You. Help us extend that love to others as we are empowered through our union with Christ. Amen."

1. Francis Dubose, "Our Life of Ministry," in *The Mission of God Study Bible*, eds. Ed Steter and Philip Nation (Nashville: B&H, 2012),1122.
2. *Heidelberg Catechism* (1563), Question 32.
3. Richard Longenecker, *Word Biblical Commentary, Volume 41: Galatians* (Dallas: Word Books, 1990), 159.
4. Ibid.
5. Kenneth Keathley, *A Theology for the Church*, ed. Daniel Akin (Nashville: B&H, 2007), 689.
6. Jerry Bridges, *The Discipline of Grace* (Colorado Springs: NavPress, 2006), 111.

> Nothing cuts the nerve of the desire to pursue holiness as much as a sense of guilt. On the contrary, nothing so motivates us to deal with sin in our lives as does the understanding and application of the two truth that our sins are forgiven and the dominion of sin is broken because of our union with Christ.[6]
>
> **JERRY BRIDGES**

NOTES

THE GOSPEL PROJECT

Session 6

Because We Are Forever

Every man must do two things alone; he must do his own believing and his own dying.[1]

MARTIN LUTHER

INDIVIDUAL STUDY

Joseph Buttom gives some startling facts about graves once located in San Francisco, CA:

> San Francisco is a city without graves. In 1900, the board of supervisors passed an ordinance prohibiting burials within the city limits. In 1912, the board announced its further intention to eliminate the city's previously existing cemeteries, and in 1914, removal notices were sent to all burial sites, declaring them a public nuisance and detriment to the health and welfare of the city.
> By 1937 the San Francisco supervisors had triumphed, and the graveyards were gone. The suburb of Colma—a two-square-mile town in which 73% of the land is cemeteries—took many of the bodies but not all. Perhaps eleven thousand corpses still lie unmarked beneath the Lincoln Park golf course, over near the coast, and the broken headstones were used as rubble in Buena Vista Park, where fragments of their epitaphs can still be read in the retaining walls and drain gutters.[2]

Growing up, how was the topic of death the "elephant in the room"?

What's the difference between saying "I'm comfortable with death," and "I'm comfortable dying"?

In this lesson, we're going to explore Joseph's story toward the end of his life. Those who truly believe in the resurrection of the dead will have a life marked by hope, joy, and promise. God's promise of eternity in our salvation is an expression of God's never-ending love for us. He loves us infinitely, so we will live eternally. In light of this promise, Christians are to believe and act on this promise, loving others in mission on their way to eternity. We don't have to be comfortable with death.

Throughout the week engage these daily study sections on your own. Each of these examines what it means to be united forever in God. There are three daily readings to prepare you before your group meets for this session. Interact with the Scriptures, and be ready to interact with your small group.

1 Prepare for Your Death

[22] Joseph and his father's household remained in Egypt. Joseph lived 110 years. [23] He saw Ephraim's sons to the third generation; the sons of Manasseh's son Machir were recognized by Joseph. [24] Joseph said to his brothers, "I am about to die, but God will certainly come to your aid and bring you up from this land to the land He promised Abraham, Isaac, and Jacob." [25] So Joseph made the sons of Israel take an oath: "When God comes to your aid, you are to carry my bones up from here." [26] Joseph died at the age of 110. They embalmed him and placed him in a coffin in Egypt.
GENESIS 50:22-26

"I am about to die." Not many young people say this. Young people think of themselves as invincible. But even if you never think about it, you could be very close to death. A car accident, a sudden heart attack, a fall down the stairs, a crime, a brain aneurysm, a heat stroke—we all know people our age who have died. Here are three different ways we deal with death—or at least attempt to mask the stench of death.

We Ignore It. The first response is to totally ignore it. Some people simply refuse to go to a funeral. They've never seen a dead body. They don't want to talk about their life-threatening disease. They don't want to put together a will or pick out a cemetery plot. The idea is too much. They say, "I just don't want to think about it." So they don't.

We can do our best to ignore death, but death doesn't leave us alone. We want to shut out the idea and think pleasant thoughts. If we can just put it out of sight, we can put it out of mind. We're like the rich fool in Jesus' story—taking into account all the space we need for big barns and harvest and money and wheat, and yet at the end, the space we need is a box to be buried in. Never taking death into account—that's one way we try to cover the stench.

We Explain It. The second way people try to cover the stench is by over-analyzing and examining death's processes. We obsess over death in its details, and we analyze its causes and effects. How many crime scene shows do we need on TV? The gory details of how the body passes from life to death, the crime scene, the analysis of dead bodies. People are intrigued about why a person dies, how a person dies, and what happens to their body after death.

Then there are shows like *The Walking Dead*, where death comes to life in the horror of zombies hungry for human flesh. These types of shows revel in the details and desensitize us to death. But death can't be contained to a flat screen or explained away by science. Eventually, you're going to be personally affected, and no amount of scientific explanation is going to satisfy you.

We Spiritualize It. The third way to mask the stench of death is to spiritualize it, to redefine it as something good, not bad. So we talk about death in peaceful terms. We say things like, "Death is a natural part of life." And we talk about death as if it's a friend, someone that's come to take us on after a long life, something we should expect and submit to. We talk about "passing away" to soften the blow. We talk about people who've died as if they're angels in the heavens or stars in the sky.

But no amount of spiritualization can take away the sting of death. To those who think death is a friend, our response should be, "Jesus didn't come to conquer a friend!" The Bible is quite clear that the wages of sin is death (see Rom. 6:23). It's the last enemy to be defeated, not the first friend to be embraced.

Which of these three responses to death resonate with you the most?

Think about the ways in which we try to avoid the reality of death. How does our culture deal with growing old or dying too young?

Joseph was prepared to die. He had lived a roller coaster life. Joseph could've died in the pit, as a slave, as a fugitive, or as a prisoner. But he managed to live a good long life.

If we're going to follow Joseph's example, we need to be prepared for death. This is something that our culture doesn't like to talk about. We don't want to think about death and the future. We do our best to screen it out. We may go visit families of loved ones who die, but we try not to think about our death. After all, isn't that kind of morbid?

But Joseph prepared for his death. He made preparations. He knew he was going to die. He was not only preparing physically. He had prepared mentally.

Preparing for our death doesn't mean we go out this afternoon and buy a burial plot, or taking out life insurance. So what does it mean? How do you keep in mind your "future death" without being morbid or negative?

2 Believe God's Promises for the Future

1 Then I saw a new heaven and a new earth, for the first heaven and the first
earth had passed away, and the sea no longer existed. 2 I also saw the Holy
City, new Jerusalem, coming down out of heaven from God, prepared like a
bride adorned for her husband. 3 Then I heard a loud voice from the throne:
Look! God's dwelling is with humanity, and He will live with them. They will
be His people, and God Himself will be with them and be their God. 4 He will
wipe away every tear from their eyes. Death will no longer exist; grief, crying,
and pain will exist no longer, because the previous things have passed away.
5 Then the One seated on the throne said, "Look! I am making everything
new." He also said, "Write, because these words are faithful and true."

REVELATION 21:1-5

In the Old Testament, Joseph knew what God was going to do. He knew that his people would be in trouble in Egypt. He knew that God was going to act decisively in favor of his family. And he told his brothers that. He told his children that. He made sure they knew what God was going to do.

Joseph believed God at His word. When God told Joseph that He was going to visit His people and lead them out of Egypt, Joseph believed that promise. Joseph knew that God keeps His promises. God had promised a certain land to Abraham and God was going to act on that.

We saw earlier that death is inevitable for all of us. That's why we should be prepared. But, like Joseph, we should also have hope. Why? Because the promise of resurrection changes everything.

The greatest gift of the resurrection is life beyond the grave. This was the hope to which Joseph looked forward. Death didn't have the last word on Jesus, and for those of us who are in Him, it won't have the last word on us either. Joseph knew resurrection was coming; death wouldn't have the last word.

What are God's promises for our future? To what extent do you believe the promise that God will wipe away all our tears?

In what ways do you look forward to all things becoming new?

The joy of the resurrection is that we'll not cease being who we are. We'll be who we are, and even more so! The life of the new heavens and new earth isn't just a shadow of this life, a wispy, cloud-like existence. The life beyond the grave is bodily.

The resurrection means that the joy of being all you were created to be—that joy will be yours. Your body will be like His. You won't be caught up in some mystical force to be depersonalized and "one with the universe." You won't be an angel on a cloud in some sort of ghostly, disembodied existence.

When Christ comes again to judge the living and the dead, He'll make us like Himself. Our final destination is a new earth. When we die, our spirits go to heaven to be with the Lord, but we've got a round trip ticket. We await the day of resurrection, when the joy of heaven is reunited with the stuff of earth. Coffins won't stay closed. Old bones will come back together. Skin will reappear. That hole we fill up with dirt will be empty once more. The stench of death will be blown away by the fragrance of new life. The cemetery is a garden, and, one day, the joy of resurrection will blow through the tombstones of all who believe!

What was the promise that Joseph believed? It was the deep, hope-filled confidence that somehow, in some way, God would make all things new. Standing on this side of the cross, we believe that in Jesus, the pain of this present world will somehow, in some way, be swallowed up by the beautiful joy of eternal life.

How does the resurrection give us joy beyond belief, the kind of joy that lasts forever and undergirds our lives?

3 Act On Your Belief in God's Promise

[24] Joseph said to his brothers, "I am about to die, but God will certainly come to your aid and bring you up from this land to the land He promised Abraham, Isaac, and Jacob." [25] So Joseph made the sons of Israel take an oath: "When God comes to your aid, you are to carry my bones up from here."

GENESIS 50:24-25

[19] Moses took the bones of Joseph with him, because Joseph had made the Israelites swear a solemn oath, saying, "God will certainly come to your aid; then you must take my bones with you from this place."

EXODUS 13:19

The third thing Joseph did was he acted on God's promise. He didn't just say he believed something; he showed it. He not only believed in what God was going to do; he acted on it. He told his family to take his body with them. He wanted that land too. Read Genesis 50:25. Now read Exodus 13:19. See? They did what he asked!

You might have heard of the story of the town that was praying so hard for rain. There was a drought, much like what many towns go through during the summer months. And all the people were praying for rain. The next day, everyone went to school and work as usual. But one little girl put on her raincoat and galoshes and took her umbrella. And everyone thought she was weird. But she said: God's going to make it rain.

Joseph's story is sort of like that little girl taking her umbrella. He doesn't just believe God. He acts accordingly. It's not enough to believe that the justice of God will flood the earth as the waters cover the sea, we must anticipate that future day even now.

It's amazing, but when the New Testament looks back at Joseph's very eventful life—a life filled with faithfulness to God and His covenant—the New Testament doesn't mention Joseph's faith when he was in the pit, when he was a slave, when he was in jail, when he was in the famine. The New Testament mentions Joseph's last words.

By faith Joseph, as he was nearing the end of his life, mentioned the exodus of the Israelites and gave instructions concerning his bones.

HEBREWS 11:22

How is Joseph a model of faith, and how can we be like him?

It's not enough to wait until the end of your life to get close to God. You should be looking for God now. Don't wait for your deathbed to get things right with God and other people. Don't live your life like it's hell, so that heaven will be such a grand leap. Start living your life with heaven in your horizon now, so that when the time comes for you to die, it's just like crossing a small threshold. Your life should be such a foretaste of heaven that your transition is as seamless as possible.

If you had to make one change so you could start living for the coming reality of heaven, what would it be?

How should we go about living our lives now in order to get a glimpse of heaven?

GROUP STUDY

Warm Up

Martin Luther, the Reformer from the 1500s, preached a sermon almost 500 years ago called "A Sermon on Preparing to Die." Here is some of what he said:

> In the hour of his death no Christian should doubt that he is not alone. He can be certain that a great many eyes are upon him: first the eyes of God and of Christ himself, for the Christian believes his words and clings to his sacraments; then also the eyes of the dear angels, of the saints and of all Christians.[3]
>
> What more should God do to persuade you to accept death willingly and not to dread but to overcome it? In Christ He offers you the image of life, grace, and salvation so you won't be horrified by the images of sin, death, and hell. Furthermore, He lays your sin, your death, and your hell on His dearest Son, vanquishes them, and renders them harmless for you.[4]

The way we prepare for death is first by preparing spiritually. What comes next after we trust that Jesus' death on the cross will cover our sins?

In what ways does preparing this way transform your heart?

Discussion

Try to ignore it, explain it, or spiritualize it—but death is still there. The gaping hole in the ground that swallows up our loved ones is real. The gaping hole in your heart as someone you love is suddenly gone is real.

You can't tie a ribbon to death. A nice little bow won't suffice. The women might have felt good by bringing spices to anoint the body of Jesus, but their spices could do nothing to change the horrible situation. Death is final, and dead people stay dead. We may feel better by covering the stench, but we can't change the outcome, as much as we might try.

Praise God we have hope in Christ's resurrection. Through it Christ has done everything necessary to deliver His people from death and ruin. The resurrection of Christ guarantees the resurrection of all believers. He will raise them just as He was raised.

During this time you will have an opportunity to discuss what God revealed to you during the week. Listed below are some of the questions from your daily reading assignments. They will guide your small-group discussion.

1. Growing up, how was the topic of death the "elephant in the room"?

2. What's the difference between saying "I'm comfortable with death," and "I'm comfortable dying"?

3. Which of those three responses to death resonate with you the most (from day one)?

4. Think about the ways in which we try to avoid the reality of death. How does our culture deal with growing old or dying too young?

5. Preparing for our death doesn't mean we go out this afternoon and buy a burial plot, or taking out life insurance. So what does it mean? How do you keep in mind your "future death" without being morbid or negative?

6. What are God's promises for our future? To what extent do you believe the promise that God will wipe away all our tears?

7. If you had to make one change so you could start living for the coming reality of heaven, what would it be?

Conclusion

San Francisco's ban on "dead people" might seem weird to you, but it serves as perfect evidence that this is the sign of our times. We don't want to see death, hear about it, or deal with it.

Your life gets its significance from where you are going; your life gets its richness from what has gone before you. How we live is important only if we see the future flowing toward us—beginning, always, with the fact that we will die and must prepare our children to assume the burdens of culture.

Spend some time praying this for you and for your group:

> "God, teach us how we should live the most meaningful life—moment by moment. Allow death to be an anchor, and let it remind us constantly that there is something out there bigger than ourselves. Let us keep in mind that we should live our lives to the fullest. Amen."

1. Martin Luther, as quoted in the Christian Classics Ethereal Library, accessed July 17, 2014. Available online at *http://www.ccel.org/ccel/luther.*
2. Joseph Bottum, "Death and Politics," *First Things*, June 2007, accessed July 21, 2014. Available online at *http://www.firstthings.com/article/2007/06/001-death-politics.*
3. Martin Luther, *Martin Luther's Basic Theological Writings*, 3rd ed. (Minneapolis: Fortress Press, 2012).
4. Ibid.
5. Charles Spurgeon, "Though He Were Dead," *Sermon*, September 14, 1884. Available online at *http://www.spurgeon.org/sermons/1799.htm*

> There is an essential difference between the decease of the godly and the death of the ungodly. Death comes to the ungodly man as a penal infliction, but to the righteous as a summons to his Father's palace. To the sinner it is an execution, to the saint an undressing from his sins and infirmities. Death to the wicked is the King of terrors. Death to the saint is the end of terrors, the commencement of glory.[5]
>
> CHARLES SPURGEON

NOTES

SMALL-GROUP TIPS

Reading through this section and utilizing the suggested principles and practices will greatly enhance the group experience. First is to accept your limitations. You cannot transform a life. Your group must be devoted to the Bible, the Holy Spirit, and the power of Christian community. In doing so your group will have all the tools necessary to draw closer to God and to each other—and to experience heart transformation.

GENERAL TIPS:

- Prepare for each meeting by reviewing the material, praying for each group member, and asking the Holy Spirit to work through you as you point to Jesus each week.
- Make new attendees feel welcome.
- Think of ways to connect with group members away from group time. The amount of participation you have during your group meetings is directly related to the amount of time you connect with your group members away from the group meeting. Consider sending e-mails, texts, or social networking messages encouraging members in their personal devotion times prior to the session.

MATERIALS NEEDED:

- Bible
- Bible study book
- Pen/pencil

PROVIDE RESOURCES FOR GUESTS:

- An inexpensive way to make first-time guests feel welcome is to provide them a copy of your Bible study book. Estimate how many first-time guests you can expect during the course of your study, and secure that number of books. What about people who have not yet visited your group? You can encourage them to visit by providing a copy of the Bible study book.

SMALL-GROUP VALUES

Meeting together to study God's Word and experience life together is an exciting adventure. Here are values to consider for small-group experiences:

COMMUNITY: God is relational, so He created us to live in relationship with Him and one another. Authentic community involves sharing life together and connecting on many levels with others in our group.

INTERACTIVE BIBLE STUDY: God gave the Bible as our instruction manual for life. We need to deepen our understanding of God's Word. People learn and remember more as they wrestle with truth and learn from others. Bible discovery and group interaction will enhance spiritual growth.

EXPERIENTIAL GROWTH: Beyond solely reading, studying, and dissecting the Bible, being a disciple of Christ involves marrying knowledge and experience. We do this by taking questions to God, opening a dialogue with our hearts, and utilizing other ways to listen to God speak (other people, nature, circumstances, etc.). Experiential growth is always grounded in the Bible as God's primary revelation and our ultimate truth-source.

POWER OF GOD: Processes and strategies will be ineffective unless we invite and embrace the presence and power of God. In order to experience community and growth, Jesus needs to be the centerpiece of our group experiences, and the Holy Spirit must be at work.

REDEMPTIVE COMMUNITY: Healing best occurs within the context of community and relationships. It's vital to see ourselves through the eyes of others, share our stories, and ultimately find freedom from the secrets and lies that enslave our souls.

MISSION: God has invited us into a larger story with a great mission of setting captives free and healing the broken-hearted (see Isa. 61:1-2). However, we can only join in this mission to the degree that we've let Jesus bind up our wounds and set us free. Others will be attracted to an authentic, redemptive community.

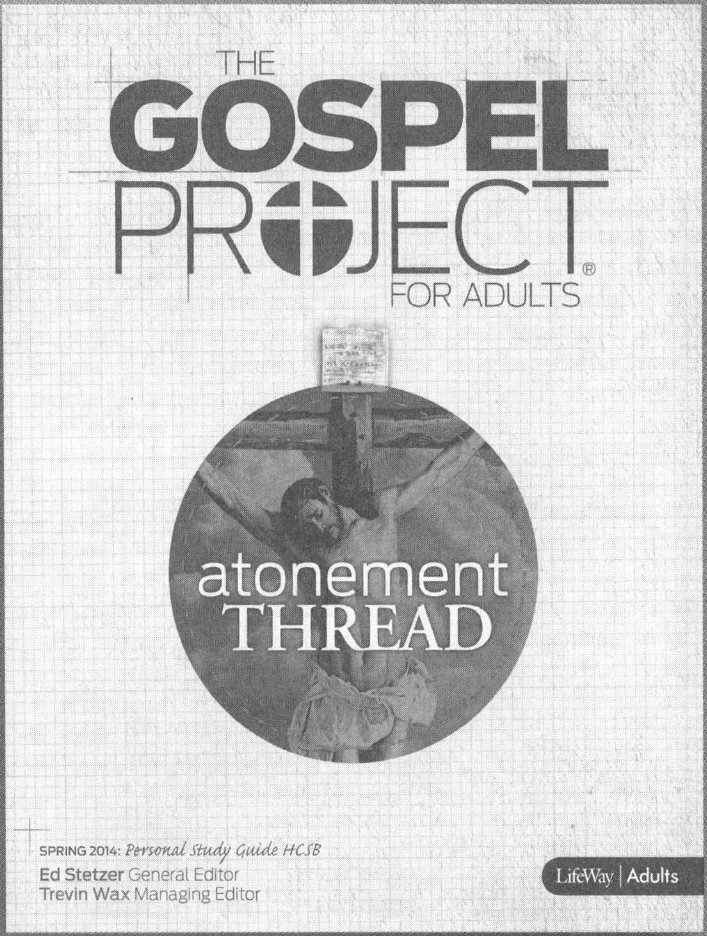
THE
GOSPEL
PROJECT®
FOR ADULTS
atonement
THREAD
SPRING 2014: Personal Study Guide HCSB
Ed Stetzer General Editor
Trevin Wax Managing Editor
LifeWay | Adults